ASTROLOGY & MONEY:

What's Your Wealth Quotient?

Also by Beverly Flynn

Astrology & Weight Control: The Jupiter/Pluto Connection

ASTROLOGY & MONEY:

What's Your Wealth Quotient?

by

Beverly Flynn

TLH PUBLISHING COMPANY

Library of Congress Card Number: 2004095233

ISBN: 978-0-9758583-1-8

First printing July 2004

Published by:

TLH PUBLISHING COMPANY
1845 Cambria Avenue
Landers, CA 92285

Printed in the U.S.A. by
Morris Publishing
3212 East Highway 30
Kearney, NE 68847
1-800-650-7888

TABLE OF CONTENTS

INTRODUCTION

If you stopped anyone on the street and asked them to name their top three wishes, money, love or health would probably be the most often heard requests. In this book, I have chosen to focus on money, as its pursuit occupies so much of our time and energy. People kill for it and obsess over it.

There have been many books written on the subject, but this book looks at it from a different perspective. The first half of the book does concern itself with the material side of money. In fact, there is a test to take which weighs several astrological "wealth factors" gleaned from studying the charts of wealthy people. By analyzing your Wealth Quotient, you can determine whether or not you are likely to earn a large income, the probability of winning a huge sum at some point in your life, or the odds of your being lucky enough to marry into wealth. Advice is given on how to improve your chances of earning a lot of money, such as the most opportune time to search for a job or start your own business, and what things to look for in your chart before buying lottery tickets or investing in the stock market.

The first part of the book is a practical, down to earth, and brutally honest assessment of your monetary situation. By comparing your calculated Wealth Quotient with others of known wealth, you can, once and for all, see if you have what it takes astrologically to amass the kind of wealth you desire. You can see what is holding you back, whether you should continue to pursue a quest for material wealth and, if so, how to go about it, or if you should consider going on to something else entirely.

The second half of the book, though, deals with the subject of money on a higher plane. We will explore the true meaning of money, and/or resources, and how to use the power of thought and attraction to bring into your life all the money or resources you will ever need to fulfill your goals. You will be invited to challenge all of your preconceived notions about money. You will learn how a goal can be the representation of money itself, and how to define the goal so clearly that the resources necessary to achieve it will automatically appear.

Finally, we will look at some of the mythological, metaphysical and esoteric lessons related to the pursuit of money passed down to us over the centuries, studying cases such as King Midas from Greek mythology and Job from the Bible. The last chapter in the book invites you to retake the Wealth Quotient test, only this time, incorporating all of the newly acquired knowledge regarding the true significance of money.

The purpose of this book is to investigate not only the tangible, ostensible qualities of money, but also the metaphysics, or the underlying meaning as well, and to learn how to use astrology in that process. Astrology has been my love for many years mainly because it forces us to look past the obvious into the subtle and to learn from studying the subtle, the essentials that will enable us to live fuller lives. Thoughts about money, how to get it, what to do with it, and who has it, permeate our world. Money is of major importance. We all have opinions about it and its use. Money is important, and something so important has to have a deeper, esoteric meaning, otherwise it would not hold such a great power over so many of us. What is this power and where does it come from? And why has it remained so important for so long? These are the types of questions I hope to answer in the second half of the book.

Our investigation begins and ends with astrology. The beauty of astrology is that not only can it tell us who is likely to have money and who is not, but it can also tell us why. It is up to us, then, to use this information wisely, after having viewed it in both an objective and subjective way. The answers to all of our questions are indeed out there. We just have to know where to look to find them. *"Astrology & Money: What's Your Wealth Quotient?"* is a complete study of money, and once you have read it, your concept of and relationship to money will be altered forever.

PART ONE

AM I GOING TO BE RICH?

CHAPTER 1

THE NATAL CHART – THE KEY TO WEALTH

I may as well break the bad news to you right from the start. If wealth isn't written in your natal chart, then you probably are not going to be rich. But having said that, there are many, many ways that wealth can be indicated in your horoscope, so do not despair. You just need to study your astrological chart a little bit to see what potential you possess and how to make the most of it. You know the old saying about there being more than one way to skin a cat? Well, that adage applies to attracting money to ourselves as well. I will prove this to you in Chapter 3 when we look at some charts of wealthy people, but for now, you'll just have to take my word for it. There are many different factors involved in making money and the more factors that show up in your birth chart, the greater are your chances of becoming wealthy.

There are two main paths to wealth, namely, we either earn it, or we get it from others, usually through inheritance, winnings, or marriage. There are, of course, a few other ways of obtaining wealth, and while unorthodox methods of obtaining money will be considered here, illegal methods of obtaining wealth are beyond the scope of this book. Also, if you inherited money or know that you are going to in the future, you probably don't need to read this book, at least not Part One, so I will not spend as much time talking about that form of attracting money, although it is included in the Wealth Quotient. Most of you are interested in earning, winning or marrying your wealth and so that is where we will spend the greatest amount of time and energy.

Wealth, just like anything else we dream about, starts from within, and astrologically speaking, this means your natal chart, because this is where we find out what basic traits and qualities we brought with us when we were born. In fact, your natal horoscope tells many things about you. It is the blueprint of your life; the foundation or framework to which everything that occurs in your life is attached. If the basic structure for wealth and prosperity is not to be found in your birth chart, then there is nothing for the desired wealth to hold onto.

To better understand this concept, consider the analogy of a woman who wants high cheekbones for a more glamorous look. Her muscles and skin are in excellent condition, and yet she is miserable because she doesn't have the hollow, high-cheek boned look of her favorite fashion model. She is well aware that the only way to achieve this look naturally is to be born with the right bone structure, for the skeletal make-up of the face determines the way the muscles and skin drape it. She can use cosmetics to give the illusion of high cheekbones, but it is only an illusion, and every night when she removes her make-up, the illusion is gone.

Now, because of the strides that have been made in the field of plastic surgery, you may be saying to yourself that this woman could just have cheek bones implanted and achieve, through modern science, the look she so desperately desires. And you would be correct in this case and you would have proven that our analogy only goes so far, because you cannot hire a doctor to change your stars. The horoscope you were born with is the only one you will ever possess; it is all that you have to work with in this lifetime. You can learn how to use it to your best advantage, but you cannot alter it.

Your horoscope, then, tells everything about your financial possibilities and your attitude towards money in general. Your chart will indicate if you are only mildly interested in money, if you have a tremendous desire to be wealthy, or if you would be happiest living in the wilderness with no possessions at all. Believe it or not, not everyone is interested in money or material things. For instance, if you have a Pisces Midheaven or Neptune in your sixth house, you might only be interested in helping others, and could care less about money or possessions except how they could help you in your efforts to help others. However, if you have Pluto in your second house, or Mars in Taurus, making a lot of money is usually on your mind and you will tend to expend much energy in its pursuit. But just because you have the desire to make a lot of money does not mean that you are necessarily going to be able to do it. Desire without the appropriate money-attracting qualities or traits in your chart means that you will probably lead a very frustrating existence because no matter how hard you try, you cannot fulfill your dreams. In this situation, probably the best thing to do would be to change the nature of your desires, but this is a topic for Part Two of this book. Right now, we just want to make sure that we have a clear understanding of the connection between the basic chart and the possibility of subsequent wealth.

Now, this doesn't mean that if you don't have any wealth indicators in your chart that you will never have any money. Even if you scored an absolute zero on the Wealth Quotient test in Chapter 3 (which is nearly impossible), you would still have opportunities for getting your hands on money through transits and progressions. The problem is, though, it probably won't be as much money as you'd like, and it probably will only be temporary. You see, transits to your natal chart by the wealth planets or their helpers can give you many, many opportunities for obtaining money, and you most likely will be able to turn some of those opportunities into large additions to your bank account. But, unless you have something in your chart that says it is going to stay, the money will slip through your fingers. This can happen in a number of ways. As a matter of fact, the universe can be very creative in coming up with ways to separate your from your money. You could, for example, be one of those unfortunate people who always seem to have an emergency or financial crisis as soon as any new money arrives. You might win $500 in the lottery only to have your car's transmission die the same day. Or, you could have a spending problem and blow all the cash in a one-day shopping spree, or you could be a compulsive gambler, etc. You get the point.

If you receive a windfall and you are going to be able to hang onto it, it will show up in your natal chart. To understand this idea a little better, let me give you a few examples along with the astrology behind them. Your nephew, John, won $100,000 in the lottery last year while Jupiter, the planet of luck, was transiting his eighth house and trining his 8th house ruler. The eighth house has to do with, among other things, lottery winnings. But when you talked to him last week, he wanted to know if he could borrow $500 from you. You asked him what happened to the lottery winnings, and he said that he had invested in a business deal that went belly-up. It turns out that your nephew has a very badly afflicted Saturn and Saturn rules his 8th house. Although

Jupiter was trining Saturn when he won the money, once Jupiter left the scene, the underlying natal horoscope took precedence again, and as a result, his joint business ultimately failed. John also has a penchant for gambling, indicated by the trine of his natal Jupiter and Mars. This tends to make him optimistic and not afraid to take chances. Mars, though, squares his natal Saturn, which as you already know, rules his 8th house, so even though he likes to take chances with money, most of the time he should not.

Another example is the case of the person who seems to have so much of the right things going for him or her, and yet cannot ever get a break. Your niece has a degree in finance and has had the worst luck when it comes to holding down a job. She seems so very nice, bright and competent, and yet has not been able to keep any job longer than six months. She has been laid off because of downsizing, fired because of a jealous supervisor, and let go because the company failed. An examination of her second house of earned income reveals that Uranus is the ruler, and as a result, her employment is a very volatile, unstable area of her life. In addition, Uranus squares her second house Moon, so that her earning ability will most likely be unpredictable and precarious. Now, there can be other factors which can mitigate an unstable second house, however, in her case, she has none, and so one would not expect her to ever have a stable income from working. Her eighth house, though, the other money house, shows a little promise and it is possible that she may marry well enough to eliminate any worries about her financial security. Since Jupiter is located on the cusp between her seventh house of marriage and eighth house of partnership income, her matrimonial prospects look very good indeed.

The above described niece and nephew are both good examples of how our basic astrology plays out in our lives, and hopefully they clarify the idea of how the natal chart lies at the bottom of your current financial situation. When we are born, we are dealt certain financial cards, and though we can sometimes do things to improve our hand, we can never escape it. Many of us try, though, and are usually disappointed. We have to learn how to use the energies in our chart in the best possible way, and sometimes that way may not be to create wealth. If you feel that some people seem to have all the financial luck, yet you seem to always fail no matter how hard you try, perhaps you need to be a little more realistic about your strengths, weaknesses, and your life's purpose.

What about the power of positive thinking, I hear you asking. What about prayer, or just plain luck. I'm sure you can think of many examples of people who were in desperate financial straits only to have some wonderful event happen to them that changed their lives, or examples, you may argue, of people who didn't give up, people who prayed, or lived right, and were finally rewarded. What about those people who intuitively knew that they were going to be successful, who held onto their dreams no matter what anyone else said. In all those cases, you will undoubtedly see an indication of money in the natal chart; the possibility of success was written in their horoscope. The fact that it took a while to manifest is just a matter of timing, which again, will be indicated in the horoscope. I am not saying don't give up hope. But I am suggesting that you be realistic about what you have to work with, so that you don't waste your life praying for something that will not happen. Your time could be better spent doing the things that you should be doing, and making progress in those areas. Study your astrological chart and learn your weaknesses and strengths. Then use your strengths to your advantage and work on eliminating your weaknesses. Also, by studying your strengths, you may discover that the reason you are failing financially is simply that you need to take a different approach to the situation. In other words, you may have the necessary astrological energies to be wealthy, and you may be using them incorrectly, or you may not be using them at all.

Before going on to the wealth indicators, a word needs to be said about identical charts. An argument can be made that astrology is not the key factor in determining wealth or anything else because two people can be born at exactly the same time on the same day in the same hospital, and therefore have the same natal charts and the same planetary energies, yet one becomes wealthy and the other does not. Why is that, you ask? Does that prove that there is more to wealth than just the stars?

Yes, there are other factors. The first of them has to do with the degree of spiritual development of the two persons involved. Depending upon our level of spiritual "maturity," we respond to the energies of the planets in differing ways. For instance, we would all agree that drive is an important quality in achieving financial success. Mars is a planet that bestows personal drive and desire, and Mars in one of the money houses could indicate a strong interest in making a lot of money. But it can also indicate someone who is using that personal desire and drive for a different purpose, such as the pursuit of spiritual "gold" or moral or spiritual values. Same horoscope, different motivations.

Here's another example. The ability to trust in the goodness of the universe, to believe that there is a higher, universal purpose behind all things, has a direct relationship to the kind of life that we manifest and is in direct proportion to the degree of spiritual evolution of the person involved. Another way of saying this is that some people are more optimistic than others, simply because of where they are spiritually. So if two people have Neptune in the tenth house of career, for instance, one could be at a point spiritually where he can only respond to the lower level Neptunian energies, and is therefore unclear and unfocused as to his career, while the other person, who is a little more spiritually evolved, can use the higher level Neptunian energies to see the vision of his ideal job and can, optimistically and with complete trust, follow that vision and achieve it.

Secondly, we all come here with our own baggage, that is, our own personal karma. We have biological karma, familial karma, national karma and spiritual karma to deal with, and in each particular lifetime, we may be focusing on a different area. Again, going back to our two babies born on the same day in the same hospital at the same time, the stars could be the same, but they could play out quite differently. In both charts, the energy potential is there to do the same things but maybe the two babies don't want to do the same things. Maybe one wants to make a lot of money, but the other wants to pursue something else. We all have different psychological motivations because we all have different karmic pasts.

Everyone's chart is full of gold, but not all of it can or should be measured monetarily. After all, there are many kinds of wealth. Remember that when you assess your chart. In Part One of this book, we are only looking for the astrological signs of material wealth and assessing whether or not we have them in our chart. If it turns out that you do, in fact, have the potential for wealth, and you want to be wealthy, then that is a plus for you. But if you don't have very many wealth indicators, then perhaps you have other, equally important psychological factors motivating you in this lifetime.

CHAPTER 2

THE WEALTH PLANETS, SIGNS, HOUSES & ASPECTS

I explained earlier that there are many factors that can contribute to wealth, which is a good thing for us. Can you imagine if there was only one specific aspect, or only one particular planet in one particular house that bestowed wealth, and either you had it or your didn't? Fortunately, the laws of the universe do not work that way, and since astrology is the study of these universal laws, it doesn't work that way either. So the very first rule to understand about wealth indicators is that there is no single indicator of financial success. The indicators are many and varied, and they show up in an astrological chart in numerous and assorted combinations of planets, houses, signs and aspects. To prove this, in Chapter 3 we will look at charts of many well-known, financially successful people and you will see that they all have different planetary combinations. They share some common indicators, but no two of them have exactly the same indicators, and yet, they all score very highly on the Wealth Quotient test.

Secondly, if an important trait or characteristic is indicated in a chart, then it is usually reinforced in many different ways. In the chart of a wealthy person, you may see, for instance, Venus, which is one of the wealth planets, in the second house of earned income. This placement alone is an excellent sign of financial success in one's career. And you may also see Jupiter, another wealth planet, in a positive aspect (conjunction, trine, sextile) to the Midheaven, also an indication of a financially successful career. In that same chart, the Vertex appears in the sixth house of work, also trining the Midheaven, indicating a certain destined or fated quality to the achievement of worldly success and prominence. It is as if the universe is guaranteeing wealth for this person by giving him many wealth and success indicators so that if one is missed, there are still several more waiting in the wings. It's a failsafe system, akin to backing up your computer. If you have the potential to be rich, the universe makes sure that you don't miss that fact.

Third, certain planetary combinations and placements are more significant than others, so they are given more importance, or weight, when determining your Wealth Quotient. As you read about the various wealth planets, houses and signs, you will begin to understand why. Certain planets, aspects and houses are considered primary indicators because their mere presence in a chart indicates monetary success, while others are secondary indicators because they don't bring fortune by themselves, and need to be coupled with other primary markers to have an influence.

So, starting with the planets, let's take a look at the wealth indicators. First and foremost, there are three planets that have the most to do with accumulating wealth. They are Venus, Jupiter and Neptune. Favorable placement of these three planets, or favorable aspects to these planets in your natal chart will almost always insure material prosperity. Sometimes even unfavorable aspects bring financial blessings, as these planets are the attractors and givers of the universe. In traditional astrology, Venus and Jupiter have always been known as the greater benefics, meaning that they give benefits wherever they are located. And Neptune is the higher octave of Venus, so it is also considered a fortunate and auspicious planet.

While it is true that Venus, Jupiter and Neptune do benefit whatever area of your life that they touch, there is much more to them than just being benefactors. They each have specific, individual "personalities," very different and specific modus operandi, and most importantly, very different and specific purposes. Each of these planets must be considered from the standpoint of its individual "personality," its method of operation, and its purpose. When added together, these three parts equal the unique quality of the planet, and in the case of our three wealth planets, it is this unique quality which makes them responsible for the accumulation of wealth. All three planets are different, and yet all are wealth generators. I will discuss each of these wonderful planets in detail, starting with Venus.

VENUS

The key word or quality relating to the planet Venus is attraction. Venus is magnetic and therefore it attracts. Wherever it shows up in your chart will indicate what it is that is being attracted. If Venus is in your seventh house, for instance, it is attracting a suitable marriage or business partner. In your eleventh house, it attracts friends. If Venus makes positive aspects to the Sun, Moon or Ascendant, or if Venus is in the first house, then this person is usually very attractive physically, since the first house governs your physical appearance. A person who is considered physically beautiful can very easily "attract" others to him or herself.

The words attraction and magnetism are used interchangeably when discussing Venus, and yet there is a subtle difference in meaning. The idea of attraction implies the power or ability of a person or object to pull or draw someone or something to it. Magnetism, on the other hand, includes this attractive function, but in addition implies the idea of some sort of force field around the person or object, so that whatever is drawn to it is trapped within this force field, making the concept of magnetism seem a little more powerful than just plain attraction. In other words, if something is magnetic, it can hold its captive for as long as it desires. So just as a pretty girl can bat her eyelashes and attract the attentions of all the young men at the dance, she must also be magnetic in order to retain their interest for the entire evening. Venus can do both.

Venus has three main areas of concern: love, beauty and money. If Venus is well aspected or prominently placed in your chart, you should be able to attract and/or magnetize all three without too much effort. So if you are interested in attracting money and more importantly, holding onto it, having Venus placed in one of the money houses, or favorably aspecting one of the rulers of the money houses would be a very auspicious wealth indicator.

JUPITER

The characteristic of Jupiter that relates most closely to the topic of this book, the accumulation of wealth, is that of beneficence. Jupiter symbolizes generosity. Whatever it is that Jupiter is handing out, it hands out lots of it. Normally we think of Saturn as being the planet that relates to karma, but Jupiter is also connected to karma, indirectly, because it is the planet that bestows blessings for past good actions.

In a natal chart, if Jupiter is found in the fifth house which rules children, for instance, the person will probably have lots of children or be very creative in some way. If Jupiter is located in the ninth house, the person could do a lot of traveling to foreign lands, or she may be very involved in publishing and thus write a lot of books, both ninth house issues. So it is quite obvious, then, that if Jupiter is located in one of the money houses, or positively aspects the ruler of one of the money houses or planets, then the symbolic significance of this is that Jupiter is going to hand out a lot of money.

Jupiter doesn't have quite the same magnetic powers of Venus so that it doesn't attract money to itself per se. But it is powerful in the area of wealth because its basic nature is that of abundance. By this I mean that its quality, which we defined above as the combination of its "personality," method of operation, and specific purpose, all combine to give Jupiter the ability to bring abundance to the area of your chart that it touches. In the Wealth Quotient calculation, Jupiter is given as much weight as Venus, because even though it lacks the same attractive ability, it still ranks very high as a wealth marker if it is auspiciously placed or aspected. Jupiter is equal to Venus when it comes to planets one would like to see in one's money houses.

NEPTUNE

Neptune is the third of our wealth planets. Neptune, as I explained earlier, is the higher octave of Venus. This implies that Neptune has all of the qualities of Venus in addition to others specific only to Neptune. Neptune is magnetic or attractive just like Venus, but on a higher, more inclusive level.

Your level of spiritual development and maturity determines what you will encounter with Neptune, so while some of you with an auspiciously placed Neptune will attract material wealth, others of you may attract things of an even higher, spiritual nature as well, so for that reason, Neptune is very welcome in our Wealth Quotient calculation.

Venus, Jupiter and Neptune are the major or primary wealth producing planets, but there are two other planets I want to discuss. I call them the "helper" or secondary wealth planets because even though they are not as powerful as Venus, Jupiter and Neptune in delivering wealth, they can aid in its accumulation if other factors are present. The two helper planets are Saturn and Mars.

SATURN

Saturn is considered a secondary wealth planet because of its ability to make things concrete, or to give them form. A person with a strong desire to make a lot of money stands a much better chance of success if Saturn is involved in some way. Symbolically, Saturn can make the dream or desire real, or concrete.

Saturn also implies a karmic connection, i.e., rewards for right actions and punishments for inappropriate or irresponsible actions. So if Saturn positively aspects any of the wealth planets, this could imply that wealth is due to that particular person as a reward for good karma earned in the past. Saturn brings with it the idea of reaping or harvesting fruits and riches based upon seeds of good planted earlier, such as hard work, responsibility and discipline.

Still, by itself, Saturn does not guarantee wealth, but if it is in positive aspect to one of the primary wealth planets, or rules one of the money houses or the Midheaven, your chances for success are greatly improved.

MARS

Mars is considered a secondary wealth planet because it represents strong desires and the energy to pursue those desires. Just like Saturn, Mars by itself does not bring wealth, for it is neither attractive nor benevolent. But because it gives the energy and vitality to achieves its goals, if its goal is the acquisition of wealth, it will allow for its aggressive pursuit. So, if Mars is placed in one of the money houses, or rules one, or is in positive aspect to one of the primary money planets, watch out.

Next, I want to discuss the houses that are most closely related to wealth. They are the second, eighth, and twelfth houses. The first two are obvious, but you may be scratching your head when it comes to the twelfth house. Why, some of you are asking, is the twelfth house related to money? Well, read on.

SECOND HOUSE

The second house is related to earned income and possessions. Any money that we receive or possessions that we accumulate are related to this house. Whether or not we will be able to earn a lot of money depends on the status of this house, the planets located therein, and the aspects made to those planets and also to the ruler of this house. The second house is of paramount importance in assessing your wealth potential.

EIGHTH HOUSE

The other natural money house is the eighth. This house relates to unearned income, that is, money you receive from others. Inheritances, alimony, lottery winnings, bank loans, joint partnership income, or any money that comes your way that you did not personally earn or that you did not earn alone. If you marry a wealthy spouse, this is also related to the eighth house.

TWELFTH HOUSE

The twelfth house is not traditionally considered a money house, and yet I am listing it as one. That is because of its relationship to Neptune, the most attractive and magnetic of the planets. Neptune rules the twelfth house, and as such, this house is the place where this magnetism or attraction can occur most powerfully. One of the traditional names of the twelfth house is the house of hidden treasures and like Neptune, its planetary ruler, the treasures of this house can be those of monetary wealth, but they can also be other things, depending upon the person and their level of spiritual maturity. That's why this house, even though not traditionally considered a wealth house, is included in the Wealth Quotient calculation.

Just as there are primary and secondary wealth planets, there are primary and secondary houses. The houses just discussed, the second, eighth and twelfth, are the primary houses. The secondary houses are the tenth, sixth and fourth.

TENTH HOUSE

The tenth house has to do with one's career and profession. It stands to reason, then, that if you are very good in your profession, that you would reap the benefits, which would more than likely include a commensurate salary. That is why, even though the tenth house is not a money house, it is related indirectly to the amount of money one can potentially receive and therefore is included in the Wealth Quotient calculation. If any of the wealth planets are located in the tenth house, or positively aspect it, or if the ruler of your tenth house aspects the wealth planets, then your chances of becoming wealthy are greatly improved.

SIXTH HOUSE

The sixth house relates to your routine work and your daily area of service. While the tenth house has more of a connotation of one's true life calling, the sixth house represents the place where you do the mundane, everyday work in support of your calling. If, however, you do this routine work very well, then just as with the tenth house, you can be well compensated for your efforts. So, if your sixth house is positively aspected, or is packed with fortunate planets, or if the ruler of the sixth house is favorably located, then you can reasonably expect to earn a good level of income for your services.

FOURTH HOUSE

The fourth house is included as a secondary wealth house because of its relationship to one's family and therefore to familial inheritance. If money planets are found in the fourth house, or if the ruler of this house is auspiciously located or aspected, this can be an indication of inherited wealth.

Neither the tenth, sixth or fourth houses are rated as highly as the primary money houses, but they do have an important role in wealth creation. Also, there is a natural grand trine formed between planets found in the second, sixth and tenth houses in the natural zodiac. A grand trine involving these houses is a magical formula for financial success based on one's work and/or career. So if there were a relationship between these three houses in your chart, there would be a natural flow between the work that you do and the money that you receive for it, and this is taken into account in the Wealth Quotient calculation also. Another natural grand trine occurs when planets are found in the fourth, eighth and twelfth houses. This grand trine is related to other people's money and your family, so if it shows up in your chart, it could relate to inherited money or wealth. This favorable combination is also included in the Wealth Quotient calculation.

Next, let's take a look at the money signs. There are three main money signs, just as there are three main planets and houses. They are probably obvious because all are related to the planets and houses we have already discussed. The three main money signs are Taurus, Scorpio and Capricorn. Let's briefly take a look at each of them.

TAURUS

The sign of Taurus stands out as the preeminent money sign. It is ruled by Venus, one of the money planets, and it is an earth sign, meaning that it is tied to things that are tangible and material. Taurus is the sign of desire, and one of the things it desires most is lots and lots of material things. And because its ruler is the magnetic planet

Venus, and because it is the sign on the cusp of the second house in the natural zodiac, it usually is able to fulfill its desire for money and possessions. Taurus is drawn to money. If the sign Taurus is strong in your chart, you will usually associate with wealthy people, you will be drawn to money and it will be drawn to you.

CAPRICORN

This is the second most important money sign. Capricorn does not have the attractive qualities of Taurus. It makes our list, though, because it is ruled by Saturn, the planet that makes things concrete. Add to that the fact that it is an earth sign, tying it to the material and tangible, and you have a very fortunate sign for accumulating wealth. If you have any of the wealth planets in Capricorn, you increase your chances of being able to put your hands on a lot of money. Also, if Capricorn is the sign on your Midheaven, or rules your second or sixth house, you are probably achievement oriented, and would therefore have a better chance of earning a lot of money from your career.

SCORPIO

Scorpio is a water sign, but it receives its ranking as a primary wealth sign because of its relationship to the eighth house. You already learned that the eighth house is of primary importance because it is related to unearned or joint income. Scorpio is the sign on the cusp of the eighth house in the natural zodiac so eighth house issues can operate very freely in this sign. Any wealth planets located in this sign would receive an added boost in power, especially where joint finances are concerned.

In addition to these three primary money signs, there are three secondary money signs, Pisces, Cancer and Virgo, and the reason for their inclusion in the Wealth Quotient calculation is explained below.

PISCES

Pisces qualifies as a secondary money sign because it is ruled by the most magnetic of the planets, Neptune, and Venus, the other magnetic planet, is exalted here. Also, it is the sign on the cusp of the twelfth house in the natural zodiac, the house of hidden treasures. If Pisces is strong in your chart, then you are probably very magnetic and if you have wealth planets placed in this sign, or the ruler of one of the money houses is in this sign, your potential for finding and/or drawing wealth to yourself is very strong.

CANCER

Cancer qualifies as a secondary wealth sign because Jupiter, the planet of abundance, is exalted here. Cancer can also play a part in inherited wealth, because of its relationship to the fourth house.

VIRGO

Virgo makes the list of secondary money signs simply because it is an earth sign and therefore closely tied to the fixed, material and tangible of which money is a prime example. Also it is the sign that rules the sixth house, one of the secondary wealth houses.

WEALTH ASPECTS

Next, I want to discuss aspects and how they relate to wealth. First, though, I would like to do a quick review of what an aspect is, and then define the basic aspects. An aspect is a geometrical relationship between two planets or a planet and an angle. (The four angles are the Ascendant, Nadir, Descendant and Midheaven. They mark the cusp of the first, fourth, seventh and tenth houses, respectively, and are considered to be very important points in an astrological chart.) The main aspects are the conjunction, opposition, trine, sextile, square, semi-sextile and inconjunct.

The conjunction occurs when two planets or a planet and an angle occupy the same degree. The trine occurs when two planets or a planet and an angle are 120 degrees apart. The opposition is 180 degrees, the sextile is 60 degrees, and the square is 90 degrees. With the semi-sextile, the relationship between the planets and/or angles is 30 degrees, and it is 150 degrees for the inconjunct.

In dealing with the major aspects and wealth, if planets or angles are in aspect to the wealth planets, then there is an influence on your ability to attract wealth, whether the aspect is a positive or negative one. As long as the planets are in aspect, there is a relationship, or a connection between them and that is all that is necessary for the Wealth Quotient calculation. Conjunctions are the most powerful of all the aspects, because they represent the combined power of two planets. Therefore, conjunctions are given more weight in the Wealth Quotient than the other aspects. The trine, sextile and semi-sextile are all favorable, with the trine being the best because it brings benefits without your having to do anything, while the sextile and semi-sextile require a little effort on your part. The square can become a positive it the person learns how to overcome the obstacle it represents, and the opposition can be overcome through compromise. The inconjunct is considered an aspect of adjustment, and is therefore similar to the square and opposition, although not as difficult.

PLANETARY AND HOUSE RULERS

Finally, a brief discussion of rulers is appropriate since they are an important part of the Wealth Quotient calculation. The following are the traditional astrological ruling planets of the natural horoscope, i.e., the horoscope that starts with Aries on the cusp of the first house.

Sign	House	Ruling Planet
Aries	First	Mars
Taurus	Second	Venus
Gemini	Third	Mercury
Cancer	Fourth	Moon
Leo	Fifth	Sun

Virgo	Sixth	Mercury
Libra	Seventh	Venus
Scorpio	Eighth	Pluto
Sagittarius	Ninth	Jupiter
Capricorn	Tenth	Saturn
Aquarius	Eleventh	Uranus
Pisces	Twelfth	Neptune

In addition to the natural or traditional rulers, we also need to consider the rulers of your personal horoscope. Obviously, most of us will not have Aries as the sign on the cusp of the first house, so unless we are Aries rising, we will need to figure out the planets which rule the money houses in our personal chart. If these rulers are located in the house in which they rule, they are given additional weighting in the Wealth Quotient calculation.

Also, if a money planet is located in a money sign or a money house, then you would expect it to have more financial power there than in other houses, therefore this situation is given a very high weighting in the Wealth Quotient calculation. If the primary money planets, Venus, Jupiter and Neptune, are found in the money signs or houses, they are weighted slightly more than having Saturn and Mars, the secondary planets in those locations, and both sets of planets are given more weight if located in the primary signs or houses versus the secondary signs or houses. Venus in the second house or Jupiter in Taurus, for example, can both be auspicious wealth markers when combined with other indicators.

Finally, before we go on to the actual Wealth Quotient calculation in Chapter 3, two other wealth indicators need to be discussed. I like to refer to them as the wild cards of wealth because they can raise the level of a wealth marker by their presence. These two wild cards are the Vertex and the Midheaven.

VERTEX

The Vertex is a point in the natal chart that is the equivalent of an angle. It represents a point of destiny, something fated or destined, or some action or event that eventually must be faced or dealt with. There is a feeling of inevitability about it. Therefore, if the Vertex is located in any of the wealth houses, or in aspect to any of the wealth planets, then it adds an aura of destiny or fate to the accumulation of wealth.

MIDHEAVEN

The Midheaven is critical where wealth generated from one's career is concerned. The Midheaven, as you know, is the cusp of the 10th house and is one of the four all-important angles, therefore, any planet that aspects it will have a major influence on your status. We have already discussed the importance of having a wealth planet located in the tenth house. However, the Midheaven is a more powerful point than the house itself, and therefore if a wealth planet aspects the Midheaven, the effect is quite strong.

The Nadir is the opposite of the Midheaven; they are on the same axis. If a planet conjuncts the Midheaven, it opposes the Nadir and vice versa. The Nadir represents the foundation of a person's life, and is the cusp of the fourth house. Any wealth planet especially favorable to the Nadir can relate to inherited income. Because the Midheaven and Nadir are on the same axis, and because any planet that aspects one will aspect the other, we will only include the Midheaven in the Wealth Quotient calculation, but in reality, we are including both.

I explained in Chapter 1 that we would be concentrating mostly on wealth earned through your own efforts, through marriage or other joint enterprises, or through winnings. But if you are interested in learning about your chances of inheriting money, when doing the Wealth Quotient test, pay particular attention to aspects made to the Midheaven/Nadir axis. For instance, if Venus sextiles your Midheaven, then it is trining your Nadir, and since the trine is more powerful that the sextile, the aspect is more likely to positively affect inherited rather than earned income.

So there you have it. Venus, Jupiter and Neptune are the primary money planets, with Saturn and Mars as secondary helpers. The second, eighth and twelfth houses are the primary wealth houses, with the tenth, sixth and fourth houses playing a secondary role. Taurus, Capricorn and Scorpio are the primary money signs, with Pisces, Virgo and Cancer being secondary signs. All aspects to money planets are significant, with conjunctions being the most powerful. Planetary sign and house rulers are also taken into consideration and weighted accordingly. And then there are the two wild cards, the Vertex and the Midheaven. Now all we have to do is combine this information in a meaningful way and we will have our Wealth Quotient.

CHAPTER 3

CALCULATING YOUR WEALTH QUOTIENT

Here is the actual wealth quotient test. I have listed the basic rules so that there should be no questions regarding terms and scoring. This test is pretty self-explanatory. When you have gone through all of the items, tally up your score, and then you can compare it to the scores of some of the wealthy people whose charts are shown at the end of this chapter.

Rules:

1. You are allowed a maximum orb of ten degrees for conjunctions, seven degrees for trines, sextiles, squares and oppositions, and three degrees for semi-sextiles and inconjuncts.

2. If more than one planet placement or aspect is true for any one item, you may allot the points for each. For instance, if having Venus, Jupiter, or Neptune in the 12th house is worth 20 points and you have both Venus and Jupiter in the 12th house, then award yourself 40 points.

Wealth Quotient Test

1.Venus, Jupiter or Neptune in the 2nd, 8th or 12th house	25 pts
2.Venus, Jupiter or Neptune rules the 2nd, 8th or 12th house	25 pts
3.Venus, Jupiter or Neptune in Taurus, Scorpio or Capricorn	25 pts
4.Venus, Jupiter or Neptune conjuncts the Midheaven or Vertex	25 pts
5.Vertex aspects the Midheaven	25 pts
6.Venus, Jupiter or Neptune aspect the Midheaven (other than the conjunction)	20 pts
7.Venus, Jupiter or Neptune aspect the Vertex (other than the conjunction)	20 pts
8.Ruler of 2nd, 8th or 12th house aspects the Midheaven	20 pts
9.Ruler of 2nd, 8th or 12th house aspects the Vertex	20 pts
10.Venus aspects Jupiter	20 pts
11.Venus aspects Neptune	20 pts
12.Neptune aspects Jupiter	20 pts
13.Ruler of 2nd house is in the 2nd, 8th or 12th house	20 pts
14.Ruler of 8th house is in the 2nd, 8th or 12th house	20 pts
15.Ruler of 12th house is in the 2nd, 8th or 12th house	20 pts
16.Venus aspects the ruler of the 2nd, 8th or 12th house	20 pts
17.Jupiter aspects the ruler of the 2nd, 8th or 12th house	20 pts
18.Neptune aspects the ruler of the 2nd, 8th or 12th house	20 pts
19.Saturn or Mars in Taurus, Scorpio or Capricorn	20 pts
20.Saturn aspects the Midheaven	15 pts
21.Venus, Jupiter, Neptune or Saturn rules the 10th house	15 pts
22.Venus, Jupiter, Neptune or Saturn aspects the ruler of the 10th house	15 pts
23.Venus, Jupiter or Neptune aspects the ruler of 4th house	15 pts
24.Venus, Jupiter or Neptune aspects the ruler of 6th house	15 pts
25.Venus is in the 4th, 6th or 10th house	15 pts
26.Jupiter is in the 4th, 6th or 10th house	15 pts
27.Neptune is in the 4th 6th or 10th house	15 pts
28.The Moon is in the 4th house	15 pts
29.Mercury is in the 6th house	15 pts
30.Saturn is in the 10th house	15 pts

31.Venus, Jupiter or Neptune is in Cancer, Virgo or Pisces	15 pts
32.Saturn or Mars in Cancer, Virgo or Pisces	10 pts
33.Ruler of the 2nd house is in the 4th, 6th or 10th house	10 pts
34.Ruler of the 8th house is in the 4th, 6th or 10th house	10 pts
35.Ruler of the 12th house is in the 4th, 6th or 10th house	10 pts
36.Ruler of the 4th house is in the 4th house	10 pts
37.Ruler of the 6th house is in the 6th house	10 pts
38.Ruler of the 10th house is in the 10th house	10 pts
39.Venus, Jupiter, Neptune or Mercury rules the 6th house	10 pts
40.Venus, Jupiter, Neptune or the Moon rules the 4th house	10 pts
41.Venus, Jupiter or Neptune aspects Saturn	10 pts
42.Venus, Jupiter or Neptune aspects Mars	10 pts
43.Any planet other than Venus, Jupiter or Neptune aspect the Vertex	10 pts
44.Any planets other than Venus, Jupiter, Neptune or Saturn aspect the Midheaven	10 pts
45.Saturn or Mars in the 2nd, 8th or 12th house	10 pts
46.Mars in the 10th house	10 pts
47.Saturn or Mars in the 4th or 6th house	5 pts
48.Ruler of the 4th house in the 6th or 10th house	5 pts
49.Ruler of the 6th house in the 4th or 10th house	5 pts
50.Ruler of the 10th house in the 4th or 6th house	5 pts
51.Ruler of the 2nd, 4th, 6th. 8th, or 12th house is Saturn	5 pts
52.Ruler of the 2nd, 4th, 6th, 8th, 10th or 12th house is Mars	5 pts
53.Any planet other than Venus, Jupiter, Neptune, Mars or Saturn in the 2nd house	5 pts
54.Any planet other than Venus, Jupiter, Neptune, Mars, or Saturn in the 8th house	5 pts
55.Any planet other than Venus, Jupiter, Neptune, Mars or Saturn in the 12th house	5 pts
56.Any planet other than Venus, Jupiter, Neptune, Mars, Saturn or the Moon in the 4th house	5 pts
57.Any planet other than Venus, Jupiter, Neptune, Mars, Mercury or Saturn in the 6th house	5 pts
58.Any planet other than Venus, Jupiter, Neptune, Mars or Saturn in the 10th house	5 pts

Donald Trump (June 14, 1946, Queens, NY, 9:51 am EDT)

The real estate tycoon has Venus conjunct his Saturn in the twelfth house. Venus rules his tenth house, and semi-sextiles Mars. His Vertex is trine his Midheaven. Neptune squares the Vertex, inconjuncts the Midheaven, rules his eighth house, and is located in his second house.

Wealth Quotient: 475

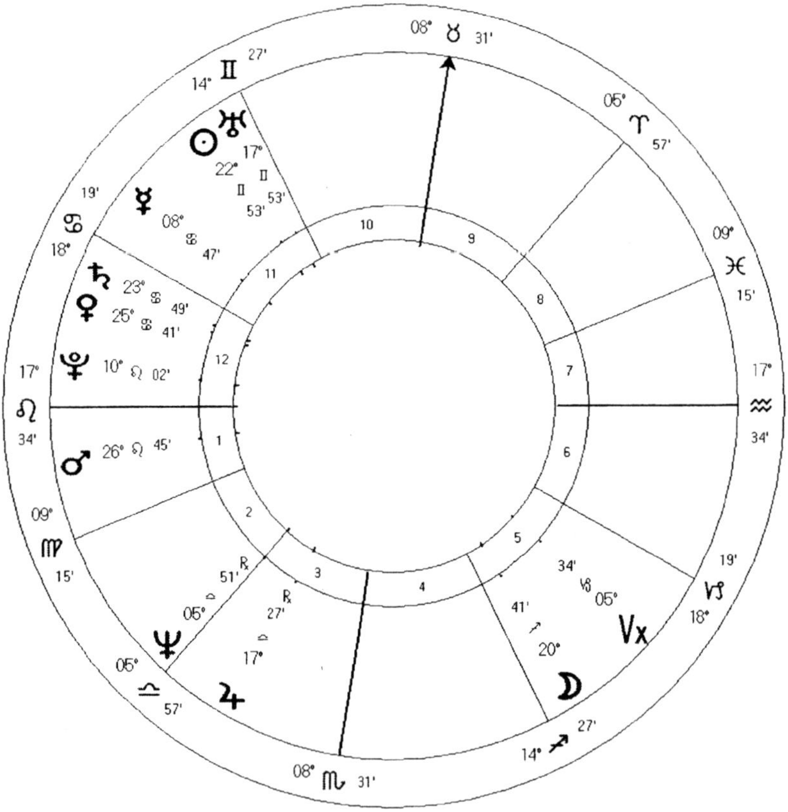

Barbara Hutton (Nov. 14, 1912, New York, NY, 2:25 pm EST)

The heiress has Jupiter conjuncting Venus, with Venus conjuncting the Midheaven. Saturn rules the Midheaven, and the Vertex squares the Midheaven. Uranus, the ruler of the 12th house, trines the Vertex and Saturn. Neptune inconjuncts Venus.

Wealth Quotient: 650

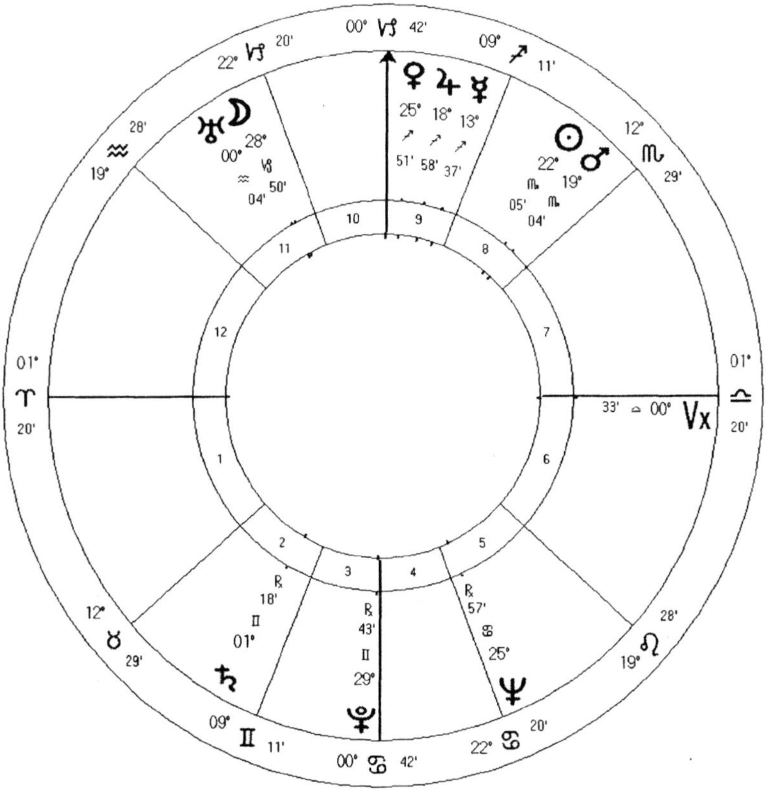

Bill Gates (Oct 28, 1955, Seattle, WA, 9:15 pm PST)

The computer wizard has Venus trining the Midheaven. Saturn also trines the Midheaven, as Venus and Saturn are conjunct. The Vertex, the point of destiny, semi-sextiles his Sun, which rules his second house of earned income. Jupiter and Neptune are sextile each other. Neptune is also the ruler of his 10th house.

Wealth Quotient: 405

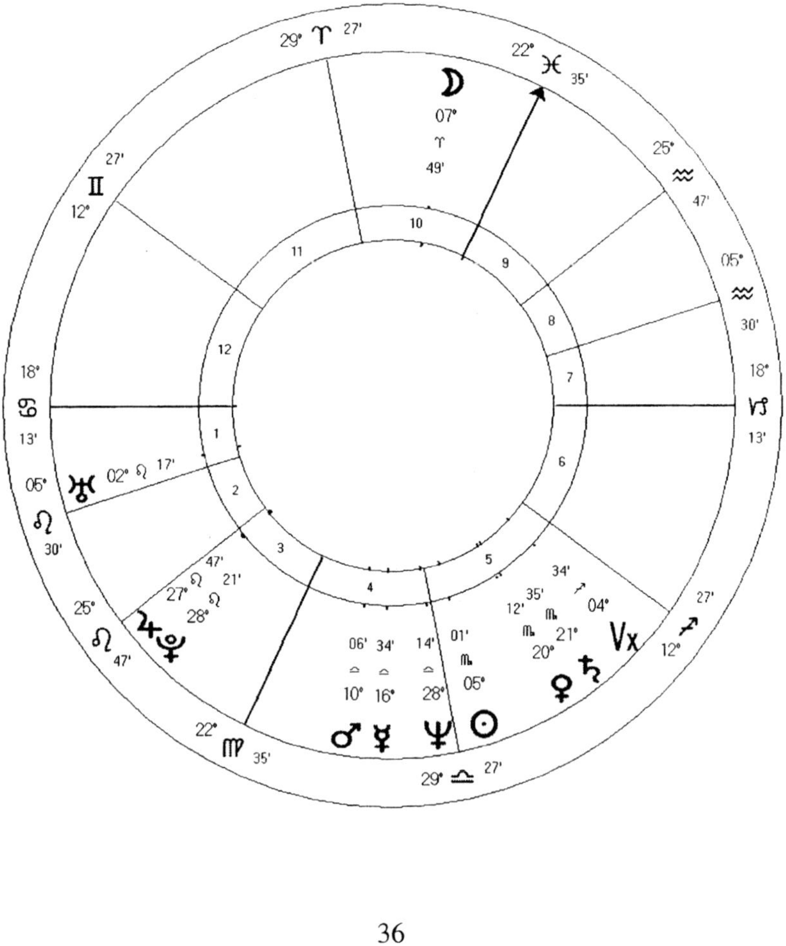

Martha Stewart (Aug. 3, 1941, Jersey City, NJ, 1:33 pm EDT)

The premier homemaker has Venus in the 10th house, and it also rules her 12th house. Mars trines her Midheaven, and Jupiter and the Vertex sextile it. Jupiter sextiles Mars, and Mars sextiles the Vertex. The Vertex conjuncts Jupiter and squares Neptune. Venus squares Jupiter. Jupiter rules the 2nd house and is located in the 8th house.

Wealth Quotient: 530

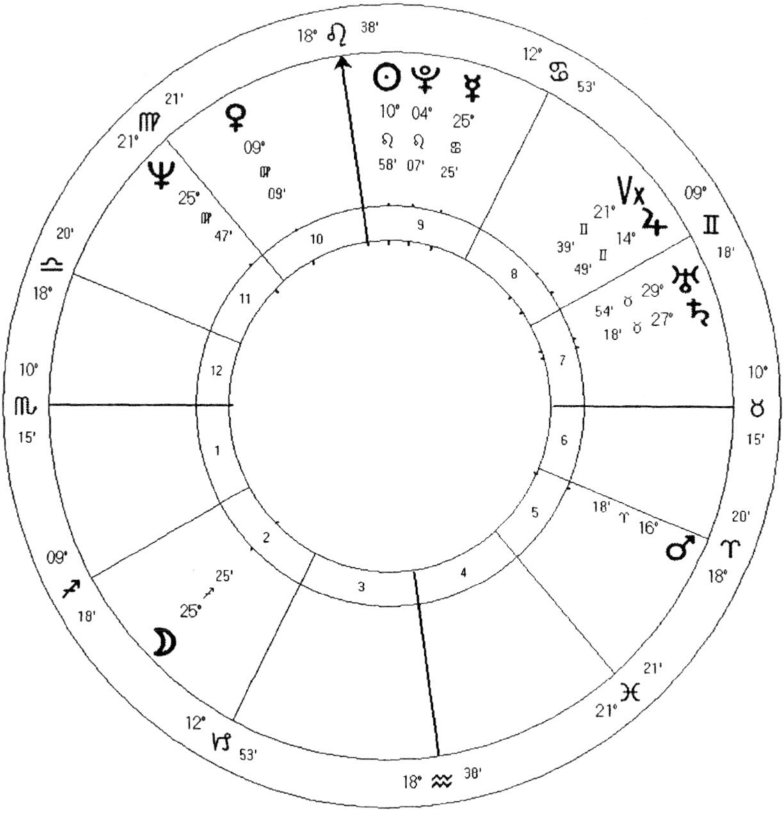

Oprah Winfrey (Jan. 29, 1954, Kosciusko, MS, 4:30 am CST)

The queen of talk shows has Neptune and Saturn in her 10th house, with Neptune conjoining the Midheaven. Jupiter trines the Midheaven from the 6th house of work. The Sun, the ruler of her 8th house, is located in the second house of earned income, conjoining Venus, the ruler of her 10th house of career.

Wealth Quotient: 590

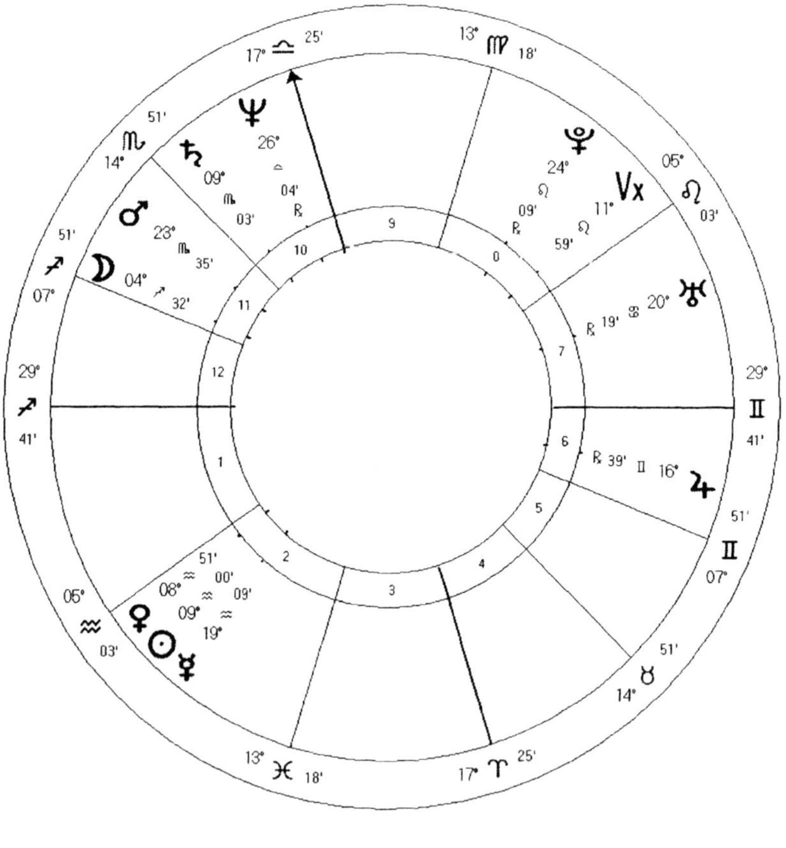

Elvis Presley (Jan. 8, 1935, Tupelo, MS, 4:35 am CST)

The King has Venus in the second house, Venus trining the Midheaven, and the Vertex sextiling the Midheaven. Saturn rules the second house, Venus rules the sixth house, and Virgo rules the Midheaven. Pluto, the ruler of his twelfth house, is located in his eighth house, conjunct the Vertex. Saturn and the Moon, the second and eighth house rulers are conjunct. Mars is in the 10th house.

Wealth Quotient: 585

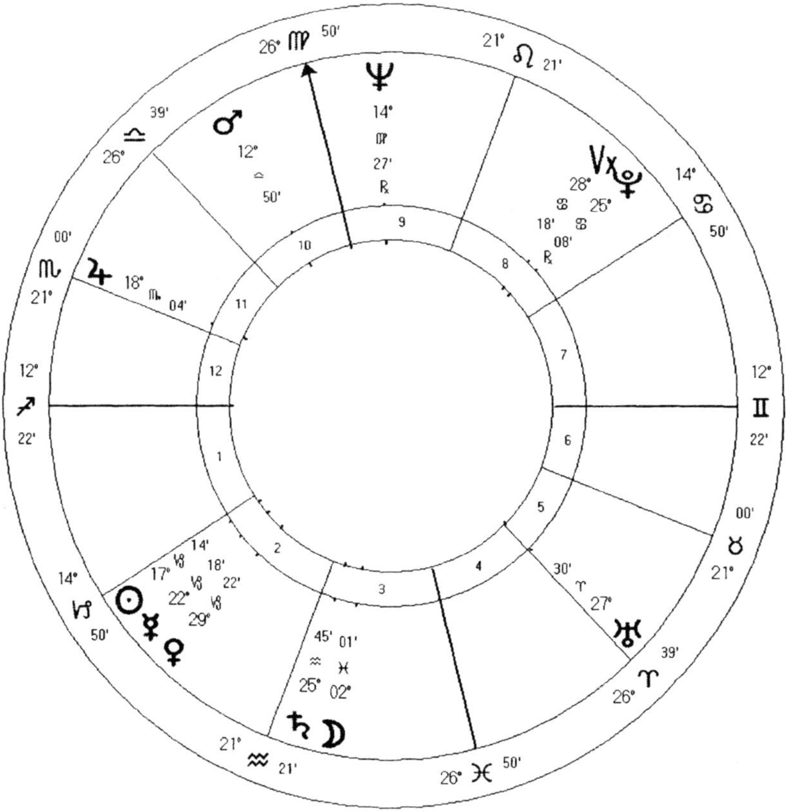

Ted Turner (Nov. 19, 1938, Cincinnati, OH, 8:50 am EST)

The Vertex conjoins Pluto, trines Venus and sextiles the Midheaven. Pluto also sextiles the Midheaven. Jupiter is in the second house and aspects Venus and Neptune. Neptune conjuncts the Midheaven, and Mars and the Moon are in the 10th house.

Wealth Quotient: 710

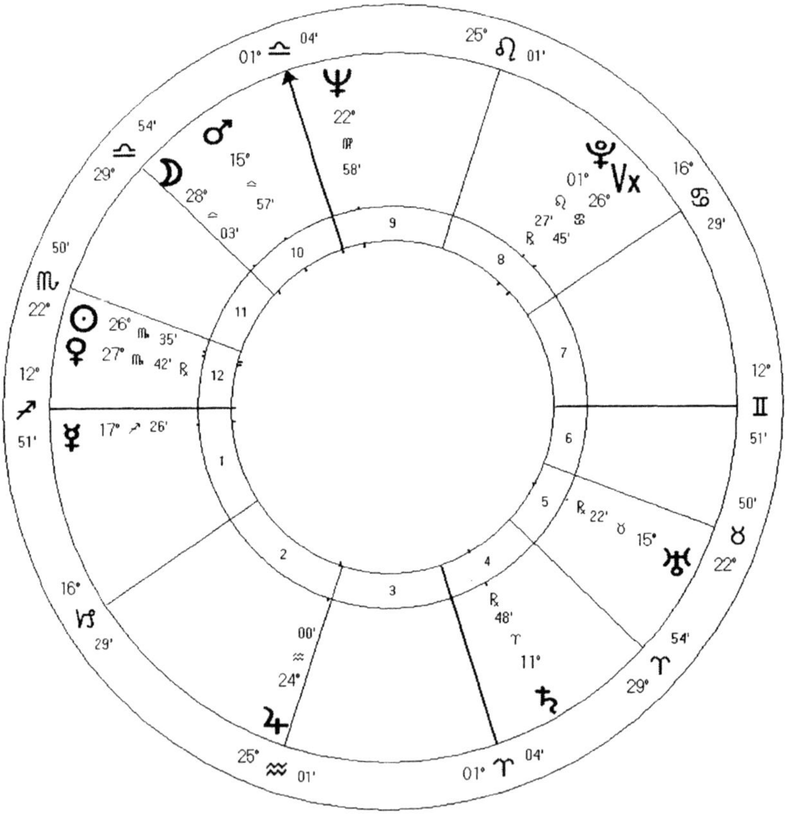

Ross Perot (June 27, 1930, Texarkana, TX, 5:34 am CST)

This wealthy Texan has Venus in the 2nd house. Neptune rules the Midheaven and aspects Jupiter. The Vertex trines the Midheaven. Saturn is in the 6th house. Jupiter, ruler of the 6th house, conjuncts the Sun, ruler of the 2nd house, and both are located in the 12th house.

Wealth Quotient: 530

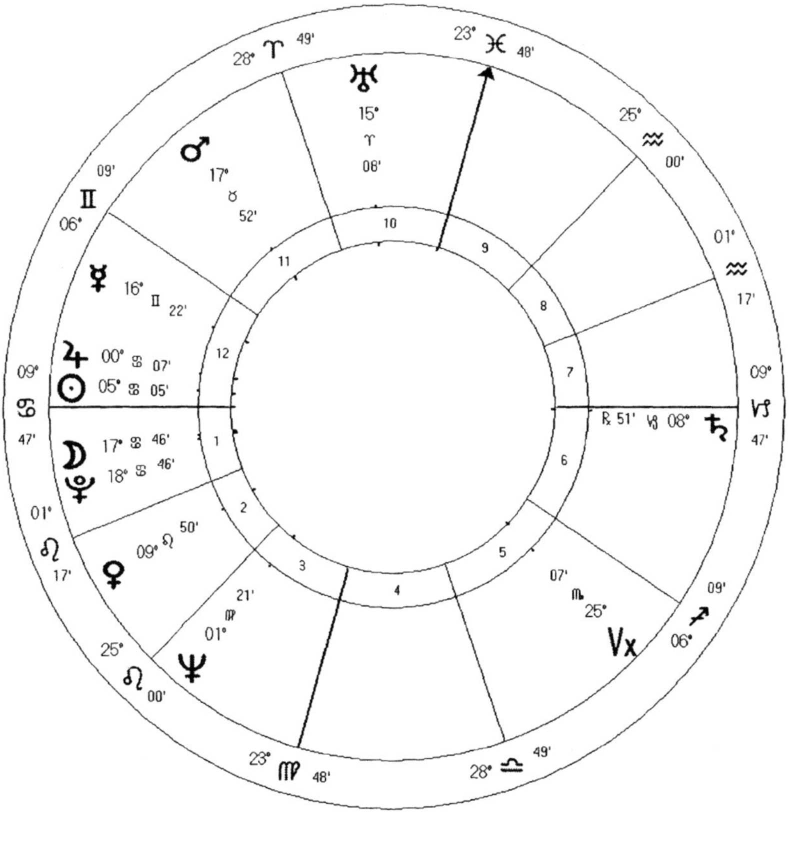

Rupert Murdoch (Mar. 11, 1931, Melbourne, Aus.,11:59 pm AEST)

The media tycoon has Neptune conjunct the Midheaven, Venus is the second house, and Mars in the eighth house. Neptune and Jupiter are sextile and Venus and Neptune are inconjunct. The Moon, ruler of the eighth house, is in the twelfth house. Saturn and Mars aspect the Vertex.

Wealth Quotient: 475

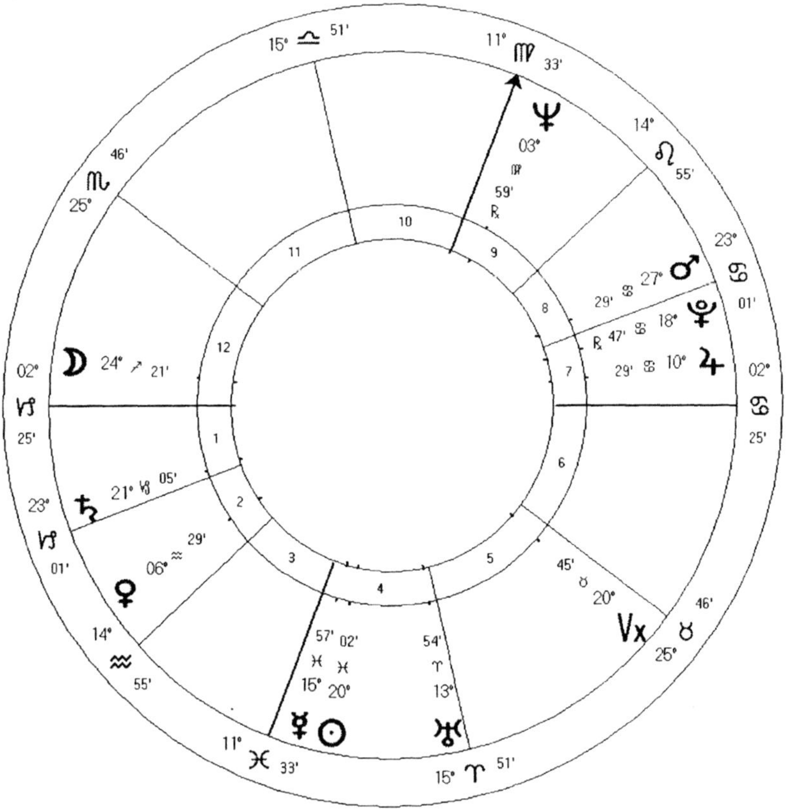

John Fitzgerald Kennedy (May 29, 1917, Brookline, MA, 3:00 pm)

President Kennedy has Saturn and Neptune conjunct the Midheaven. The Vertex sextiles the Midheaven, conjuncts Jupiter, and semi-sextiles Venus. Venus, ruler of the 8th house, is placed in the 8th house, along with the Sun, Jupiter, Mercury and Mars.

Wealth Quotient: 690

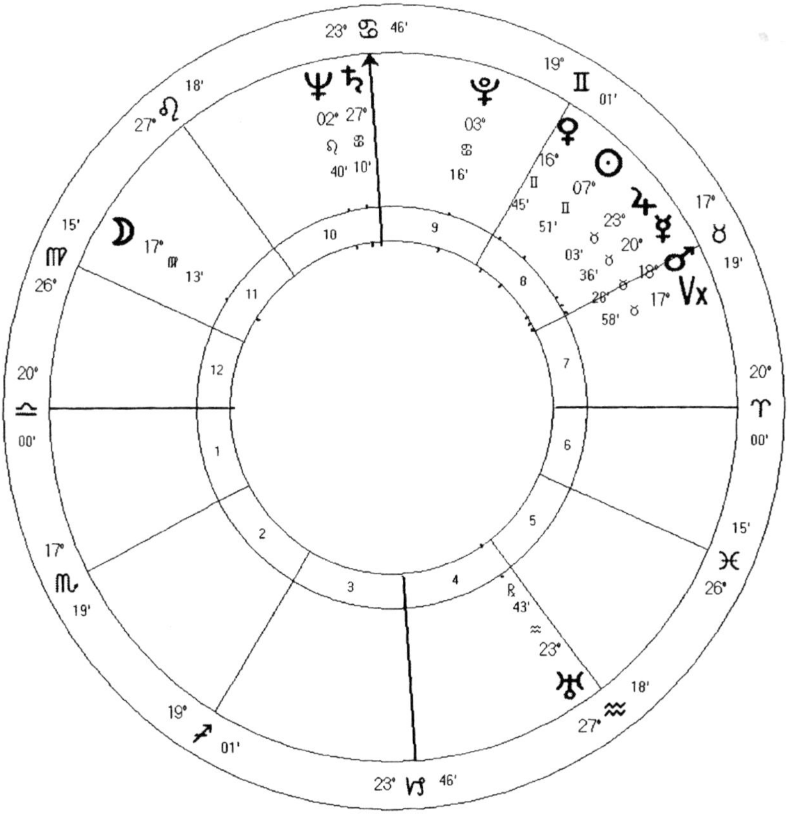

Queen Elizabeth II (Apr. 21, 1926, London, England, 2:40 am BST)

The Vertex sextiles the Midheaven and Saturn conjuncts it. Mars conjuncts Jupiter, and both square Saturn and the Midheaven. Her eighth house ruler, Mercury, is located in her second house, which Neptune rules.

Wealth Quotient: 525

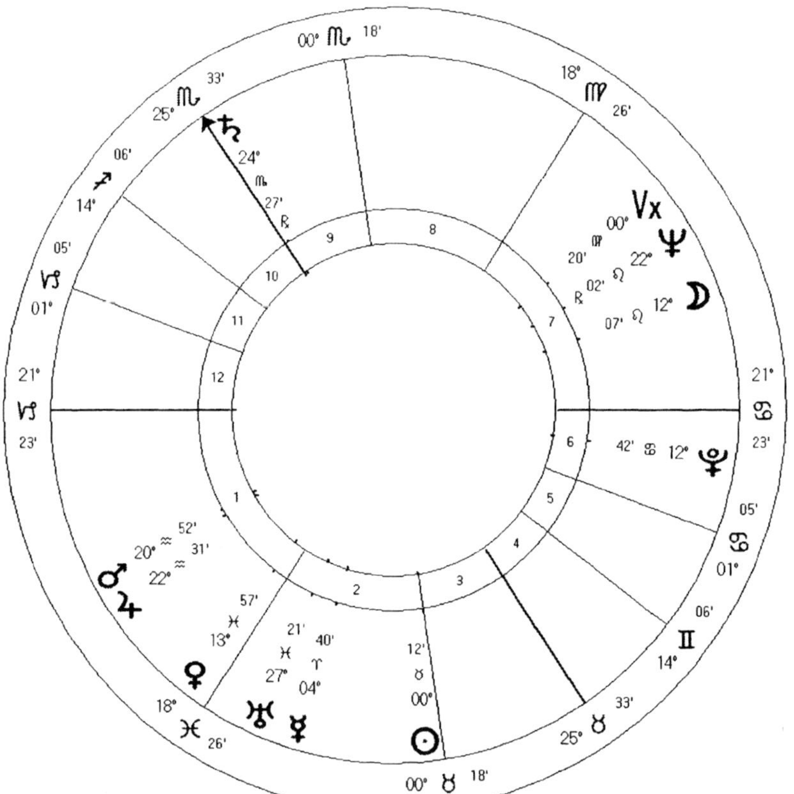

CHAPTER 4

WHEN WILL THE CASH ARRIVE?

So now you have computed your Wealth Quotient, and it's much higher than you expected. (Those of you with low Wealth Quotients will be dealt with in the next chapter.) You've double-checked your calculations to be sure that you are working with the right number. You are certain that the math is correct, so now you are wondering why you are not in a better position financially. If the Wealth Quotient says you should be rich, why aren't you?

Many people who take the Wealth Quotient test ask this question. And there can be many answers. Since the test is based solely on your natal chart, one way of looking at it is that it is an indication of promise as yet unfulfilled. The imperative, then, is to determine what it is that is holding up the fulfillment of this promise. Is it simply a matter of timing, or are there other factors to be considered? Are there obstacles standing in the way of the achievement of your financial goals? And if there are obstacles standing in the way, how do you determine what they are, and more importantly, how do you eliminate them?

In many cases, the answer is simply a matter of timing. The study of astrology provides not only answers as to your basic character and the qualities you possess, but it tells you when the energies are right for certain events to happen. Most often there is nothing you can do to speed up the timing. Understanding astrology, though, will help you understand why you were required to wait for certain events, which can sometimes make the waiting a little bit easier. In astrology, the way we find out when something is going to happen, that is, the timing of an event, is primarily through the study of transits and progressions. Secondarily, we look at other factors that can play a part in timing, such as eclipses, Saturn returns, Chiron returns, the North and South

Nodes, and the Vertex.

Before we begin talking about transits and progressions, I'd like to say a few words about timing in general, and how it relates specifically to our wishes and desires. We can want a lot of things to happen in our lives, and sometimes, before we have the time to make them happen, we realize that those goals or dreams weren't what we really wanted after all, and are glad that they didn't manifest. If something is supposed to happen, there is an indication in your chart, and though you may have to wait a bit, it usually will happen. However, if you have been longing for something for quite a while and there is no indication that it is going to happen any time soon in your chart, ask yourself if this particular desire is something that you truly want or that you just think you want. Maybe it is one of those things that you will be glad one day that didn't happen. What you desire most should align with other areas in your chart such as your Ascendant, your Midheaven, and your Sun. If your wish is not in line with these three major areas of your chart, then you should reconsider why it is that you desire this particular happening so strongly. But if there are indications in your chart that what you wish or desire is in line with what should be happening, then, you can look to see if timing is the reason it has not manifested yet.

TRANSITS AND PROGRESSIONS

Transits represent the continuing movement of the planets from their position in your natal chart to the present time. So, while Jupiter may have been in Aquarius when you were born, over the next twelve years, it has traveled through all of the signs and is back where it was when you were born.

Progressions are of two main types, primary and secondary. Primary progressions are sometimes called solar arc progressions, and each degree of movement represents one year. With secondary progressions, each day's movement represents one year. Both progressions are indicative of inner growth and experience that is then manifested outwardly, while transits work from the outside in.

With transits, energies are made available to you during the transit, and will be gone once the transit leaves, so you should always take advantage of positive transits. Transits are most indicative of timing when they are conjuncting the angles, but other transits can be timing agents as well. Transits of Jupiter can bring luck in the nick of time, and transits of Saturn allow you to finally get things going, although sometimes not without a struggle. Transits of the outer planets, Uranus, Neptune, and Pluto almost always indicate a major change. If they are transiting the money houses of your chart, the second or the eighth, or if they are aspecting a planet which rules the second or eighth house, then you can expect to see something happen in the financial area of your life. If it is a positive aspect, you may finally get the help that you have been waiting for.

For instance, suppose that you started a business a year ago, and have been working very hard at making it a success. You put all of your savings into the business to get it started, but the business has not caught on, and you are concerned about whether or not you can make it another year. In examining your chart, you notice that Uranus is going to be trining the ruler of your eighth house in two months. This is a boon to your business, for you will be able to appropriate the necessary financing to keep your business afloat until it takes off. Better still, you note that Jupiter will be conjuncting the ruler of your second house of earned income at the same time, a very strong indication that your earnings are about to increase.

Here's another example. Suppose you have been struggling for many years to become an actress. You have worked very hard, and in the mean time, have been supporting yourself by working several different kinds of jobs, including sales and service occupations. You are beginning to lose hope that you will ever see your dream come true, and then one day, you get a call from your agent telling you that you have been offered a small part in a movie, with the long-awaited salary you have been hoping for. You check your chart and realize that transiting Jupiter has been hovering around your Midheaven, and that it has been trining the ruler of your tenth house as well. Your career just got its lucky break.

Progressions are similar to transits in effect, except that they usually begin their magic as an inward "feeling" or response to energies, which changes you inwardly at first, and then is evidenced in the outside world. The end result is the same as the transit; the beginning is just different.

Transits and progressions are timing indicators because the movement of a transiting or progressed planet to a different house or different sign means the end of one area of interest and the start of another. The progressed Sun moving from Cancer into Leo, for instance, marks the beginning of a thirty-year time period, when you will be very motivated to discover your true self. Progressed Venus moving from the first to the second house is an indication that your focus will shift from you to your values and how you earn a living. The progressed Moon is an especially accurate indicator of timing by showing us the area of life where we are currently emotionally focused. As an example, if the progressed Moon is traveling through your seventh house, partnership and relationship issues will form the backdrop of your emotional focus. If the progressed Moon is in the sign of Aries, there will be an aggressive, pioneering undertone to all of your feelings that will carry over into your actions that will last until the progressed Moon leaves Aries. If the progressed Moon aspects a natal, transiting or progressed planet, it acts as a signal to begin or end whatever the planet represents. Pluto, for instance, represents transformation, so the progressed Moon conjoining your natal Pluto is indicative of a transformation becoming final.

How do the transiting and progressed planets relate to financial status? First of all, if a transiting or progressed planet is moving into a money house or sign, then the activity of that house or sign is being given the signal to become active. The emphasis lasts for only a certain amount of time, but in the case of solar arc progressions, the period of time can be quite long, and so much can be accomplished. Since solar arc progressions only move about one degree per year, Venus, for instance, progressing primarily through your second house of earned income can have an effect for thirty years. That's long enough to do quite a bit of accumulating. The same could be said of Jupiter progressing primarily through your tenth house of career. You would have a thirty-year period of career expansion, which can allow you ample time to build the kind of status and reputation that should theoretically allow you to earn a substantial amount of money.

We talked earlier about the fact that usually there is more than one indicator of major changes in your life. This is especially true in the case of change caused by transits and progressions. For instance, a prime indicator of timing is a conjunction of a planet or angle with the progressed Moon. If your progressed Moon is conjuncting your Midheaven, you can safely expect your career to begin taking off. But if you see other transits at the same time that also support this, then you should pay close attention to the area of your career, for it is probably getting ready to make a major shift in direction. These corroborating transits could occur in many ways. For instance, you could have a planet transiting one of the career related houses, i.e., the second or sixth, at the same time as the progressed Moon conjunction to the Midheaven. Or, a transiting planet may be aspecting the ruler of your second, sixth, or tenth house at the same time as the planet transiting the career related house. Or, you could have a progressed Venus or Jupiter involved in some way, or maybe the progressed Vertex is conjuncting your tenth house ruler. There are many, many corroborating transits and progressions, and if you see them, realize that this is an important time in your life, because when something is important, it will be emphasized and re-emphasized in your chart.

That's why you can go for years without having anything major happen in a certain area of your life, even though planets may touch it constantly, especially the inner, faster moving planets. Your natal Venus, for instance, the number one wealth planet, is conjuncted, trined, squared and opposed by the Sun and Mercury each year. Mars, which takes about two years to complete a cycle of the zodiac, would make the same connections to natal Venus in a two year period. With all these connections, you would think that something would be happening all the time. And little things are indeed happening, but nothing major. Many planets always announce the major events.

Also, major happenings in one's life usually involve one or more of the outer planets in order to make them stick. Jupiter, Saturn, Uranus, Neptune and Pluto need to have their hand in the mix if one is to experience a significant life change. The faster moving planets help things move along, but the major push comes from the slower moving planets. Jupiter brings luck or opportunity and Saturn indicates the karmic tie. Uranus, Neptune and Pluto represent permanent change, although each has a different way of bringing that change. With Uranus, permanent change is abrupt and unexpected, with Neptune, it is subtle and invisible, and with Pluto, a major transformation unfolds slowly and with much drama. So if you want to know when to expect your financial situation to improve, look to see what major transits or progressions are occurring in your life, that is, transits involving the slower moving planets. Then check to see if there are other similar corroborating transits of the faster moving planets that support the change.

Transits and progressions of the slower moving planets that occur at the angles of the chart are another indication of a significant happening. Any time an outer planet travels through one of the four angular houses, its emphasis is increased, but especially when it first enters the house. Finally, transits by the slower moving planets of the major wealth houses and transits to the wealth planets and rulers of the wealth signs are also significant and can be indicators of major changes coming to your life in the financial area.

ECLIPSES

Sometimes called the wildcards of the zodiac, eclipses are very powerful timing factors, for they speed up the arrival of events. Eclipses create effects similar to those represented by Uranus in that they are sudden and disruptive, only more so. If an eclipse occurs in an area of our chart that we do not want to see changed, then the effect of the eclipse can be unpleasant at first. Eclipses should be welcomed, though, because they usually bring changes that are very beneficial in the long run, even though we don't always realize it at the time.

Eclipses repeat themselves about every nineteen years. They affect two signs, for they occur on the axis of a sign and its opposite. For instance, eclipses could be occurring on the Leo/Aquarius axis, or the Gemini/Sagittarius axis. They usually occur in pairs and are active for six months until the next set. Eclipses take about eighteen months to pass through each set of signs, so if you are having eclipse-related problems, know that you only have to deal with the disruptions for about a year and a half and then they will die down.

Eclipses are important in our discussion of money because if they are occurring in money signs, or if the signs are related to the money houses, mainly the second and eighth, then there is going to be some kind of activity in the financial area of our life. The activity can be welcomed or unwanted, depending on the other transits taking place in your life at the time. If the transits are basically good, then the eclipses will improve upon that. If the transits are difficult, the eclipses in that same area may appear to make things more difficult for you. If there are no major transits or progressions going on in that area, then it is hard to say what will happen. However, if the eclipses touch any of your natal planets, you may be able to determine what the effect will be based upon the nature of the aspect made, and the condition of that particular planet in your natal chart.

For instance, if during a lunar eclipse, the Moon is conjuncting your natal Mars in Taurus in the fifth house, and your natal Mars squares your natal Venus, you may see issues related to romance heating up, although the square will tend to cause problems in the area. Since eclipses speed things up, if your romance was rocky and you weren't sure whether or not the relationship was going to last, the eclipse would more than likely influence you to end it right away, thus freeing you to move on to another more appropriate relationship.

You can see now how an eclipse can work wonders in your financial life if it is active in that area of your chart. Something that may have taken a year or two to manifest may be sped up so that it occurs within days or weeks. If you observe that an eclipse will be positively aspecting the financial areas of your chart, then get ready for action. If you have been waiting to make a decision, or waiting for someone else to act, expect things to finally start moving right around the time of the eclipse. Also, if you know that the eclipse is going to be activating that area of your chart, make plans ahead of time so that you will be ready when it happens and can take full advantage of the energy. Remember that the effects of the eclipse only last about six months until the next eclipse takes place, and that you only have about a year and a half before the eclipses leave that area of your chart altogether. Eclipses are an extremely valuable tool not only for timing purposes, but also for identifying opportunities.

THE SATURN RETURN

Saturn is the planet most associated with time. Saturn is sometimes referred to as Father Time. In mythology, the story is told that Uranus, Saturn's father, represented limitless or infinite time, and when Saturn castrated his father, restricted or finite time as we know it began. Saturn, also because of its link to the karmic areas of our lives, brings another aspect to the area of timing. Sometimes we want things to happen, but before we can have what we want, certain responsibilities or duties must be handled or fulfilled. This is the basic idea of karma, a sort of balancing of the accounts. The location of Saturn in your natal chart will give you an indication of the most pressing karmic responsibility you have to fulfill in this lifetime.

Saturn assists us in fulfilling our karmic responsibilities by placing us in situations where we have the opportunity to make correct, responsible choices. This is referred to sometimes as testing. When Saturn is testing us, we are usually made aware of this by a Saturn transit or progression. If we pass the test, we usually know it, because at the end of the transit, we receive our "karmic reward." This reward is usually the accomplishment of something we had been working on achieving during Saturn's transit. If we did not rise to the challenge and did not work responsibly in the area that Saturn was transiting, then when the transit is over, the opposite effect is usually the case. We discover that we may have failed to achieve our desired goal, or we may have been humiliated in some way, or taken down a peg.

The most significant test Saturn puts us through has to do with the placement of our natal Saturn, and so whenever transiting Saturn returns to this point, it is to grade us on what we have accomplished during the twenty-nine years that it was away. That is why Saturn returns can sometimes be very difficult. They don't have to be, though, if you have been working responsibly and diligently on the issues represented by Saturn's placement in your natal chart. But if you have not made wise decisions in that area over the years, when transiting Saturn returns to its natal position, you may feel increasing pressure to do something differently in your life.

The Saturn return, then, can be quite significant where timing is concerned. The first Saturn return occurs when you are around twenty-eight or twenty-nine years old, and can mark a period where you are rewarded for your efforts. If your natal Saturn is in a money house or sign, or makes aspects to any of the money planets or rulers of your money houses, then the rewards could definitely be in that area. If you didn't quite succeed the first time around with the tests and challenges that were presented to you by Saturn, you may have to wait until the next time Saturn is active in your chart to receive your rewards. If you do have Saturn in a financial house or sign in your natal chart, and you have not received the financial rewards that you feel you are due, take a closer look at the house and sign of your natal Saturn and make sure you understand exactly what is being asked of you.

Saturn is noted for its ability to limit and restrict our movement in the particular house in which it is transiting. If that house is a financial house, and there appears to be work that has not been accomplished, then we could feel as if our financial well has dried up. A normal Saturn transit of the second house of earned income, for example, could result in your salary being cut, or maybe even being laid off from your job. When the Saturn transit of the second house is also a Saturn return, then the effects will be more pronounced for they are, in effect, a judgment and sentencing. The feeling of financial scarcity only appears if you have not met the responsibilities or learned the lessons required of you. On the other hand, if you have done what you should have done during those years that Saturn was away, the result will most likely be just the opposite. If you have made appropriate choices when asked, when Saturn returns to your second house, your income will most likely stabilize if it has been unstable, and you may receive that raise that you had been hoping for, or you may find that your income is increasing by other means. The main thing to remember about Saturn is that you will receive exactly what you deserve and what you have earned.

So if your natal Saturn is in any way related to the financial areas of your life, and you were not happy with the results that transpired at your last Saturn return, look at this as an opportunity to discover what attitudes you need to change, or in what ways you need to grow, so that you will be able to make more responsible choices the next time that you are given the opportunity to be tested by Saturn. Once you pass the test, whole new worlds of financial freedom will open up to you.

THE CHIRON RETURN

Chiron is an asteroid located between Saturn and Uranus. It was discovered in 1977. Chiron is referred to as the wounded healer. In mythology, he was a centaur, half-man and half-horse, and the son of

Saturn, which made him immortal. One day, he was accidentally struck by a poisonous arrow. The pain from his wound was horrible, but because he was immortal he could not die to escape the pain. So the gods allowed him to become mortal so that he could die and end his suffering. Astrologically speaking, then, Chiron represents the place in your life where you are wounded and need to be healed. It takes almost fifty-one years for Chiron to return to the place where it was when you were born, and this is just as significant as your Saturn return. The importance of the Chiron return is that if you are able to heal that area of your life, you can then use those energies to help others.

Since Chiron takes fifty years to return to its natal position, if it is related to your financial success in any way, the possibility exists that you may have to wait a long time for your financial rewards. This is not necessarily the case, though, for Chiron can be active in your chart at various points throughout your life. As transiting Chiron makes aspects to the other planets in your chart, it is looking for you to find the way to heal yourself, that is, to overcome the pain that you feel in that area, and then to go on to achieve something with that knowledge. If you have been able to resolve the issue where you have been "wounded" and turn it into something more powerful, then any financial results tied to Chiron can be achieved. However, if you have not been able to resolve your Chiron issues before the time of the return, you will receive an extra amount of assistance at that time.

Chiron is important in our discussion of money because if it is located in a financial area of your chart, and you are particularly sensitive in that area, then you may not do what you need to do because it hurts too much. For instance, if your Chiron is located in your tenth house of career, you may associate feelings of wounded pride, or rejection or alienation in that area of your life, and therefore, you may not pursue your career with as much vigor as you should. You may "baby" yourself in that area. The lesson of Chiron, though, is that you have to figure out a way to overcome the pain, to heal yourself, so that you can continue. And by healing yourself, you become stronger, you will reap the rewards promised by a successful healing, and you will be able to guide your life into a whole new direction.

RETURNS IN GENERAL

We have discussed the returns of two important planets and have seen their relationship to the timing of events in our lives. But returns in general should be watched. While returns of the inner, faster moving planets are not so significant, they do have a short-term effect, and a return of Jupiter to its natal position every twelve years can be quite significant because it indicates a new cycle of opportunities for progress. If your natal Jupiter is located in a money house or sign, or aspects a wealth planet, then the Jupiter return may bring with it many wonderful things related to finances.

Besides Saturn and Chiron, Jupiter is the only other slow moving planet that has returns that we need to be concerned with for timing purposes. Uranus has an eighty-four year cycle, and so its return would not have much effect on our financial life. Neptune and Pluto have even longer cycles, 165 and 248 years respectively, and so they never return to their original position in our lifetimes.

THE NORTH AND SOUTH NODES

The North Node relates to the new and pioneering direction that your life should take, and the South Node is indicative of the old direction, the area that you have already mastered. If your South Node is placed in a monetary house or sign, then perhaps your financial success is being held up until you work more on your North Node path.

What this means to us in our study of wealth is that if you have a South Node related to money, and you are pursuing it instead of the area of life represented by your North Node, then you may be blocking your ability to achieve financial success. Let's look at an example of how this works. Suppose you have the South Node in the eighth house which relates to, among other things, the resources of others. Your North Node would then be placed in the opposite house, the second house of earned income. From a strictly material perspective, having the South Node in the eighth house often indicates that you have already tread the path of relying on others for financial support and that now it is time for you to learn how to earn your own living and support others.

Pursuing the North Node direction requires courage, for it is unfamiliar territory and will take you to new, uncharted places in your life. But you have to summon the courage to try, because that is the path, which will lead to rewards. In the case of the North and South Nodes, you really do have control of the timing, for it is only when you decide that you are going to pursue your new path rather than the old one that things begin to change. So if your North and South Nodes relate to financial areas, and you feel that you are constantly frustrated in your efforts to achieve your financial goals, take a look at which path you are following, and make the necessary adjustments.

THE VERTEX

Remember when we talked about the Vertex in Chapter 2? At that time, I indicated that the Vertex operates something like one of the angles in a chart, and that it is an indicator of something destined or fated. So if wealth is in your destiny, the Vertex may have something to do with the timing of the event. Look for aspects to the Vertex from major transiting planets at the same time that other signals are showing up in your chart. Transits of any of the outer planets to the Vertex plus a shift of sign or house of a progressed planet can sometimes indicate major life changing events.

If there is a major planet aspecting the Vertex, or if an eclipse occurs near the Vertex, and your Vertex is either placed in one of the money houses or signs, or the planet it is aspecting is a money planet, then there is a possibility that some destined or fated action will occur with regard to your financial situation. Since we can calculate transits and eclipses ahead of time, you can note future eclipses and transits that will be activating your Vertex, allowing you to plan accordingly to take full advantage of them. Remember that after the transit is over, and six months after the eclipse, the effects die down, and so you must not let the opportunity pass by unnoticed or unused.

Many times, when the Vertex is activated, people come into our lives that turn out to be very beneficial or crucial to whatever we are doing at the time. Be on the lookout for those people. One of them may play a very important role in the achievement of your goal, and if your goal is financial rewards, you do not want to miss them. It may turn out that you need their help to proceed, or that they have some advice to give, or that they hold a piece of information you need before you can go to the next step in your plan. Pay extra attention if someone arrives in your life at a time when your progressed Vertex is angular, because as we discussed earlier, the four angular houses are more powerful in effect than the others. A progressed Vertex at the Midheaven, Ascendant, Descendant or Nadir is an almost certain sign that either an event or a person is coming and you have to deal with them and what they bring if you are to fulfill your destiny.

Activation of the Vertex means that we are going to be pressured internally to do something, for we feel instinctively that it is something that has to be done. But, as with everything else in our lives, we have free will and can consciously choose not to do this fated or destined thing. We can ignore the urges, no matter how strong. If we do that, though, we are impeding our evolutionary progress. Astrologers give a name to the point opposite the Vertex. It is called the Anti-Vertex, and it represents the point of freedom. In other words, if you have completed the work required by the Vertex, if you have faced your destiny, you are then released and can enjoy the point of freedom.

This is important because if achieving the wealth you desire is somehow related to your Vertex and you do not accept the challenge of the destined or fated event or encounter, then your destiny with wealth may be postponed. You may not be able to reach the point of freedom. It takes courage sometimes to reach a goal, and facing the situation brought on by the Vertex can sometimes require a great deal of courage. However, if you determine that your Vertex is in any way tied to the accumulation of wealth, they you will need to be courageous if you want to attain it.

FREE WILL: THE CHOICES WE MAKE

The last category I want to discuss regarding timing has to do with something unrelated to astrological factors. Free will, or our ability to make our own decisions and choices in our lives, has a lot to do with the kind of life we are leading today. Our horoscopes are an indication of possibility, and the transits and progressions can influence us, but they cannot make us do something if we choose not to do it. In the final analysis, we are the ones who determine our fate because we are the ones who determine whether or not we will take advantage of planetary assistance.

There are many reasons why we do not take full advantage of planetary help when it is offered to us. One reason may be that we are afraid to let something good happen to us because the trappings that go along with success may be more than we can handle. Sometimes we sabotage ourselves, or set ourselves up for failure, simply because subconsciously we really do want to fail. That way, we can say to others that we really tried, but that life was against us. And the reason that we subconsciously want to fail is because we don't know how to be happy. We have been unsuccessful for so long, that we become comfortable in that state, and the idea of changing from our comfortable and familiar position to a successful yet new and strange position is frightening enough to keep us from moving forward.

We can rationalize our way out of doing anything new or different, and I'm sure you have done so many times. I know I have. Someone offers you the opportunity to advance, and you can come up with all kinds of reasons why you shouldn't take them up on their offer. I am reminded of a very popular movie, *The Shawshank Redemption,* a moving story about prison life. One of the subjects it dealt with was institutionalized behavior. An inmate who had been in prison his entire adult life was finally released, and ended up committing suicide because he could not make the adjustment to living as a free man in the outside world. He was so institutionalized that he preferred the comfortable and familiar life of a prison inmate to a life of freedom and the unknown. On a smaller scale, many of us behave just like this fictional prisoner in that we choose to stay in our comfortable prison rather than venturing out into the free, unknown world.

The bottom line is that we can choose to be happy or we can choose to be sad. We can choose to live life abundantly with all that that implies, or we can choose to live a small, limiting life. And we can rationalize and make ourselves feel comfortable with either situation. If your chart indicates that you have the potential to be financially secure and you are not, maybe you are simply exercising your right to choose, your free will, and you have chosen a less abundant, but more comfortable existence.

This chapter is about timing, and so maybe it is time to exercise your free will in an opposite direction, in the direction of abundance and change, instead of the less abundant and familiar. This choice can be extremely difficult for some, because it is so hard to go into the unknown, even though the unknown may be a thousand times better. But implicit in the idea of free will is the idea of freedom. That means that if you are exercising your free will, which all of us are, and you do not feel free, then maybe you need to take a look at your definition of freedom. If you are defining freedom in any way that is confining or stunting your growth or your ability to pursue your dreams, then you are not defining true freedom.

Freedom means no constraints, and will means power. Free will means that you have the power within yourself to act with no constraints. You can choose to go back to school to increase your knowledge so that you can get a better job, or you can rationalize your way out of it by saying that you're too old, or that your family won't be able to survive without you. You can go on and on. Reasons for not reaching for one's future abound. But there is only one reason to reach for your future, and that is, that you want to be successful. You want to reach the potential of your horoscope. You want to exercise your free will to make decisions that will speed you towards your goal of financial success.

You may be saying to yourself that this whole discussion does not apply to you. You really do want to be financially secure. But sometimes we sabotage ourselves subconsciously, and if you have been struggling towards financial freedom for a long time and have not achieved your goal, it wouldn't hurt to do a little self-analysis to see if perhaps you are doing things that sabotage your progress. If you discover that you are, then exercise your free will and choose to behave differently the next time a similar situation arises in your life.

In summary, then, if you have a high Wealth Quotient score and your financial situation does not match the potential indicated by your score, you need to first of all determine if you have been giving your financial situation the attention it deserves. If the answer is no, then start formulating a plan and begin to actively pursue it. Get help if you need it, but get going. If you are not where you want to be financially and you are sitting around doing nothing, you have only yourself to blame.

If you answered yes to the question, that is, if you have been actively and intelligently pursuing a strong financial foundation and it has not materialized, then timing is a serious consideration, and hopefully you have learned how to locate the pertinent areas of your chart related most strongly to the timing issue. Also, you should be checking to see if there is a karmic or fated aspect to your ability to generate wealth, and are on the way to resolving any such issues. Then make sure that you are not holding yourself back by choosing the safe and familiar route over the new, the unknown and the pioneering.

Finally, a word needs to be said about patience. Patience is one of those virtues tied up with the signs most often associated with material success, the earth signs Capricorn, Virgo and Taurus. Indeed, these signs are noted for their patience, endurance and steadfastness. They instinctively know that if you want something worthwhile to manifest, you have to give it time. If you have done all that you can do to achieve your financial goals, if you have followed the rules outlined in this chapter, and you have done all of the required soul searching, then maybe you simply need to be patient.

CHAPTER 5

HOW TO IMPROVE A LOW WEALTH QUOTIENT

Now let's look at the other side of the coin. You have diligently completed the Wealth Quotient test in Chapter 3, and realize that your score is not as high as you would like. The question you are probably asking yourself is, can anything be done to improve a low Wealth Quotient? The answer is yes. Although, as pointed out earlier, you cannot rewrite your horoscope, there are some things that you can do that will improve your situation. Certain financial traits can be learned, and if practiced, can yield better results than if you had not tried them. Also, there are some mental tactics that you can use to help improve your approach to the whole subject of money and wealth, so let's take a look at a few of them.

MAKE FULL USE OF YOUR ATTRIBUTES

No matter how low your Wealth Quotient score, you must have at least one positive aspect to the wealth planets. Or possibly one of the wealth planets is placed in one of the money houses. Make an inventory of your best wealth aspects and planet placements, and then ask yourself if you are using them to the fullest. If the answer is no, ask yourself why not. If the cards you have been dealt are not all you had hoped they would be, learn to look at them in a different, more creative way, and learn to take initiative to create, or at least alter, your destiny.

For instance, suppose that you have a low Wealth Quotient score. You determine that not one single planet, or the rulers of your wealth houses are placed in any of your money houses. The aspects are almost as grim, but you do have Venus trining Jupiter. This is a wonderful aspect where money is concerned, and even though Venus and Jupiter are not in money houses, the energy of this trine can certainly be used to help enhance your financial situation. This trine bestows the ability to combine the attractive qualities of Venus with the expansiveness of Jupiter. Suppose the planets are located in the third and seventh houses, respectively. The energy, then, is related to communication and partnerships. So, one possible way to maximize this trine would be to look for ways to work with a partner to increase your wealth, in areas such as teaching, writing, or speaking. Since Venus is in the third house, opportunities for these third house issues should be fairly easy to attract, especially if you are keeping an eye out for situations involving partners. Having Jupiter in the seventh house means that partnerships will be very beneficial for you, so if someone approaches you with an idea for a book that they want to co-write with you, listen to what they have to say. And if no one approaches you, then take the initiative and come up with some joint project related to communication and approach someone who you think would make a good partner.

Here is another example. Suppose, after completing the Wealth Quotient test, you discover that you only have one good planetary placement, Venus in the sixth house. The sixth house, as you remember, is considered a secondary wealth house because it relates to your routine, daily work and if performed well, could lead to financial gains. Venus, being the planet that rules money, would be very helpful in this house, and so if you are concerned with earning a good living, you have a tremendous amount of help here. With this placement, it would be very important to analyze your field of work and make sure you are doing what you do best. Do it well, with a good attitude and though you may not become as wealthy as you'd like, you should never have to worry about your basic needs being met.

Let's look at one more example before leaving this section. Suppose that you have no aspects between the wealth planets, and no wealth planets in the wealth houses, but you do have Pluto in your tenth house. Pluto is not a wealth planet, but the tenth house is one of the houses and Scorpio, ruled by Pluto, is the sign of your Midheaven. Having the ruler of a secondary wealth house located in that house can be quite beneficial to one's ambitions, and we have seen the connection between a successful career and the related monetary rewards. So your job is to figure out how to take maximum advantage of this fortunate placement. This particular Midheaven and planetary placement would indicate that you are probably very intent on delving deeply into your career, and so would be intensely motivated to succeed. This placement of Pluto would give a tremendous amount of inner strength and focusing power as well, so if you are not focused on your career and on being a success in it, then call up that Plutonian reserve and use it. Anyone with as much resourcefulness and inner drive as this Midheaven and Pluto imply should be able to accomplish much in their chosen profession, and if that happens, monetary rewards would most likely follow.

The idea that I am trying to convey is to make maximum use of the gifts and talents you possess. You may not have received everything you wanted, but you have received something. Rather than spending time lamenting what you don't have, thoroughly exhaust those talents and abilities that you do have.

USE TIMING TO YOUR GREATEST ADVANTAGE

Someone with very few positive wealth planet placements or aspects should pay particular attention to timing. Transits and progressions should become your best friends. You need to become intimately aware of the comings and goings of beneficial transits and progressions. Trines, especially, can be wasted if we do not use them, and they can easily pass us by if we are not aware that they are happening. Timing is everything when it comes to initiating projects, approaching financiers, asking for a raise, etc. Common sense dictates that you ask for money at the most opportune moment, and the only way for you to identify the most opportune moment is by paying close attention to your transits and progressions.

For instance, if you know that Saturn is going to be squaring the ruler of your second house for the next few weeks, you might want to wait until it moves on before approaching your boss about your raise. Saturn restricts, and squares place obstacles in the way, and so you will probably run into all kinds of problems with your boss, and even if you do receive a raise during this period, it will more than likely be a lot less than you had anticipated. Saturn trining the ruler of your second house is a different story. Saturn makes things concrete and will give you what you deserve. So if you deserve a big raise, you may get one here.

The best possible scenario, though, would be to wait until Jupiter or Venus is making a positive aspect to your second house ruler, or note when either of them is going to be traveling through your second house. That would be a much more appropriate time to ask for your raise. Even if Jupiter and Venus are not in your second house or in good aspect to the second house ruler, there are other times that would be fortunate for attracting money and so you should pay attention to them. If Jupiter is aspecting your Sun or Ascendant, or traveling through your first house, you would be placed in the spotlight, so to speak, and would therefore receive a lot of positive attention, which would more than likely lead to a good outcome. All of the above applies to Venus and Neptune as well.

Pay attention to the house that Mars is transiting, for it will give you an indication of where the action is at that particular time in your life. Mars gives energy and vitality to pursue the issues of the house in which it is transiting, and so Mars traveling through the second house would be an indication that you have a lot of energy available to you to pursue the goal of getting a raise. Be careful that there are no hard aspects to Mars, though, for that may mean that you may be a little too aggressive in your approach.

We have been dealing here only with asking for a raise, but hopefully you can see how these concepts can be carried over to any area of your life. The main idea that I would like you to take with you from this discussion is that there are certain timeframes that are more conducive to achieving goals than others, and that if at all possible, you should act during these beneficial periods.

IMPROVE YOUR ATTRACTION QUALITIES

How can you make yourself more magnetic, so that you can attract what you want? We learned that Venus and Neptune are the two planets that have the most to do with attraction, so if these two planets are weak in your chart, you will probably have a more difficult time fulfilling your needs than someone with a very strong Venus. But we are going to be proactive here and initiate some actions that can hopefully shift the balance more in your favor.

When we talk about someone or something being attractive or magnetic, we can look at this from several levels. From a strictly physical level, being attractive or magnetic can mean attracting money to oneself but it can also mean simply attracting people. And on that level, there is much that can be done to make us more attractive physically. We can spruce up our wardrobe, change our hairstyle, or lose a few extra pounds. You must agree that when someone is physically attractive, they tend to be more self-confident, and they seem to receive more breaks or benefits than those who are not as attractive physically. Looking better will make you feel better. I cannot guarantee that improving your physical attractiveness will increase your chances of attracting more money, but it certainly cannot hurt them.

Next, take a look at your attractiveness on an emotional level. If you are not as emotionally open as you feel you should be, maybe you need to give some thought to making a few changes in that area. If you close yourself off emotionally, you are sending out a subconscious signal to others to stay away from you. How can you expect to attract emotional warmth and support from others if you do not send it out yourself? It doesn't take that much effort to smile a little more, to say hello to a stranger on the street, or to say yes instead of no to an invitation. Again, I cannot prove uncontrovertibly that there is a link between emotional outpouring and the attraction of wealth, but it only stands to reason that if you are able to attract others to yourself emotionally because of the warmth and support you send out, then you may be able to attract other things as well. So try it.

Finally, let's look at attraction from a purely mental perspective. How do you make your mind and your mental processes more attractive? First of all, you can take a look at how you think and use your mind. Do you need to become more organized and focused in the way you think? If you have a tendency to be scatter-brained, or if you go off half-cocked instead of thinking things through first, you may need to do a little work on improving your thought processes. If you tend to be a negative thinker, if you always think that the worst is going to happen in every situation, then you may need to develop a more optimistic mental attitude. By becoming more positive, more focused and more organized in your thinking, you are more inclined to attract others who are also more positively focused, and that in turn may attract many of the other things you want. Related to how you think is what you are actually thinking about. Do your thoughts need to be lifted to a higher level? If your mind is in the gutter, that is, if it is focused on the wrong things, then you will attract others who also are prone to focusing on the wrong things. Change what you think about and you will change the kinds of people and experiences that come into your life.

Making ourselves more attractive is something that can be done with just a little effort, and yet the payoff can be quite large indeed. Even if these changes don't bring you all the material rewards you want, they can certainly help in achieving your goal, and they may bring other things to you that you have never even imagined.

ADOPT A JUPITERIAN ATTITUDE

There is a saying that goes, "Fake it until you make it." I've always liked that saying because it conveys the idea that if you present the attitude of a winner to the world, eventually you will become one. It implies a certain amount of hope and optimism about the future. It says that even though you are not where you want to be presently, there is absolutely no doubt that the future you dream of will one day be real. In astrology, this kind of optimism and hope is represented by the planet Jupiter. Wherever Jupiter is located in your chart is where you are the most optimistic and hopeful, and are likely to be the most successful.

Jupiter is one of the wealth planets because it bestows largesse upon its subjects, largesse in spirit as well as in material things. If Jupiter is weak in your chart, or if it is poorly aspected, then you may not feel as much of this Jupiterian benevolence as those who have more powerful Jupiters. But rather than sulk, if you are not feeling particularly blessed by Jupiter, why not act as if you are and see what happens. Why not act as if you have been touched by Jupiter's beneficence, and by so doing, see if you can actually create some of that famous Jupiter luck.

Just how does one fake a Jupiterian attitude? You can start by approaching life with that big-hearted sense of joy and optimism for which Jupiter is famous. You can wake up each morning full of excitement and anticipation, knowing that whatever comes your way will be wonderful and in line with your life's purpose. Learn to see the positive side of every occurrence in your life. Develop a true sense of hope for a glorious future and a basic trust in the goodness and generosity of the universe. Tell yourself over and over again that everything is going to be great until you finally believe it.

From an astrological perspective, look at your own chart and ask yourself how things would be different if Jupiter were in a better location in your chart and then begin acting as if it were. Suppose, for instance, that Jupiter was trining your Venus instead of squaring it. Or, how would your life change if Jupiter were actually placed in your second house of earned income instead of the third? What effect would there be on your career if Jupiter were conjoining your Midheaven? Once you have come up with an answer, begin living your life as if it were so.

Let's analyze the Midheaven supposition a little. Suppose your chart has no aspects to the Midheaven, or suppose you have aspects to your Midheaven but they are all difficult squares or oppositions. Presently, you feel that you have hit a dead end where your business or profession is concerned. But imagine what your attitude would have been had you been born with Jupiter at your Midheaven. You would have been happy to go to work each day, and luck and opportunities would have followed you everywhere. So why not pretend that you are lucky anyway, and that opportunities are everywhere and you just need to find them. By changing your mindset, you just may change what happens to you.

Developing a Jupiterian attitude may take some very hard work, especially if you have had many years of practice living in the throes of negative and pessimistic thinking. But it is worth the effort, for what you believe to be true has a great bearing on what you will actually be able to achieve in your life. If you believe that you are lucky and that opportunities abound, you will see things in a whole new light, and perhaps you really will be able to create some luck for yourself. Even if you don't yet believe that you are lucky, pretend. Even if you don't believe that the universe is good and bountiful, pretend. Eventually, you will believe. And in the meantime, fake it until you make it.

IMITATE SUCCESSFUL PEOPLE

I'm sure you have heard this piece of advice before, but it is important, so I want to spend some time discussing this topic. Successful people are everywhere. They are proof that there is a secret to being successful and that they have found it. Logically, then, it only follows that if they have found the secret, so can you. So why not study their lives and see exactly what they did to arrive where they are. It makes perfect sense to attempt to figure out their secrets and then use them yourself in your quest for success.

What I am suggesting here is patterning your life after the life of someone else your respect or admire, or someone who has achieved whatever it is that you wish to achieve. Astrologically speaking, this is really a fairly simple thing to do. As a matter of fact, it is one of the reasons that astrologers spend so much time studying the charts of famous people. Their lives are usually very public, and so facts and dates of major events are common knowledge. You can use their charts to examine their basic qualities, strengths, weaknesses and motivations. Then you can compare them to your own strengths and weaknesses and see what areas you need to work on improving.

Studying the chart of a successful person can also shed light on issues of timing. It can give you an idea of how long it takes for a dream to manifest, especially if you know something about the dates when major events actually happened in the life of the particular person. Just knowing that it took someone ten years or twenty years to reach a major goal or make a dream come true should give you hope that maybe all it will take for your dream to manifest is just a little more time.

By studying the lives and astrological charts of successful people, you can learn a lot about how the energies of the planets work in an individual life, and thereby gain greater insights into what to expect when similar astrological combinations show up in your chart. For instance, if you know that your hero got his first big break when transiting Jupiter was conjuncting the Midheaven, you know to watch out for similar circumstances when Jupiter approaches your Midheaven.

By studying the lives and astrological charts of successful people, you can learn about perseverance and determination, and how they handled the bad times, how they were able to bounce back after failures, and how they learned not to give up. Sometimes you can look at your life and think that things are so bad that you will never be able to succeed, but then if you read about someone who had it worse than you and overcame greater obstacles, you feel silly for complaining about your plight.

Studying the lives of successful people can be very uplifting and encouraging, for they show us what the human spirit is capable of, and therefore, what you and I are capable of achieving. If you are having problems finding your way in life, find someone you respect and admire and try to incorporate some of their ideals into your life and that should help you get to the point of being able to develop your own ideals.

RETHINK YOUR LIFE

If, after reading all of these suggestions for improving your Wealth Quotient, you feel that nothing resonates with you, then perhaps you need to take a fresh look at your life and your goals. Maybe the reason you are striking out in the financial arena is because you have been pursuing the wrong things. You may need a career adjustment, or perhaps need to rethink your life altogether. Very often, we get stuck in a rut and the only thing that can get us out of it is to go off in an entirely new direction.

Sometimes we cannot even recognize that we are in a rut. Sometimes we are so enmeshed in the mess that is our life that we need a catastrophic event to help us extricate ourselves. Astrologically, this often happens when we have major transits from the outer planets. Uranus, especially, can create those kinds of unexpected life-altering crises. So if you see that you have a Uranus transit coming up soon, this might be a sign that you are about to be shaken up a bit, and that during that shaking up, you may realize that you, in fact, do want to make some major changes in your life.

The same thing can be said of Neptune and Pluto transits and progressions. Uranus, Neptune and Pluto all work to create major changes in our lives in order to get us in line with our basic life purpose, only they all use different methods. While Uranus creates unexpected disruptions, Neptune takes a softer approach. Neptune allows you to see the world through rose-colored glasses, that is, it allows you to see the highest and best version of yourself. And then it gradually destroys the old version, so gradually that you don't realize it is happening. So if you see a major Neptune transit or progression approaching, expect to see a different version of yourself gradually appear. Finally, Pluto likes to nudge you towards change by forcing you to confront issues that have been buried deeply in your subconscious. Pluto will bring them to the surface so that they can be eliminated once and for all, allowing you to move forward toward your newer and better self.

If you don't see any major Uranus, Neptune or Pluto transits on the horizon any time soon, you can still do a life review on your own. Take a look at your career. See how it measures up to the sign on your Midheaven. If you are not pursuing an appropriate career, you will lack the passion and drive that spurs you on to do a good job, and as a result, earn a good income. Identify the house which holds the planet that rules your Midheaven and see if that gives you any additional information as to where and what you are supposed to be doing with your life. Also, look at your second and sixth house rulers. Note their placement in your chart. Since the second house has to do with earned income and the sixth house with your daily work, they should relate positively to your career also. What you do with your life has a lot to do with the wealth and income you draw to yourself, so it is extremely important that you identify your correct and true calling.

By doing this analysis of your career houses, you ought to be able to gain some insights and determine if some changes need to be made. If, however, after all of these suggestions, you are still confused as to how to improve your financial situation, then perhaps you need to take a whole new look at money and what it really means. That is exactly what we are going to do in Part Two.

PART TWO

A NEW LOOK AT MONEY

CHAPTER 6

WHAT IS MONEY?

Money is defined in Webster's dictionary as any article or substance used as a medium of exchange, a measure of wealth, or a means of payment. Throughout the history of mankind, there has always been some kind of money, and it has taken many forms. Indeed, the history of money shows just how flexible and creative humanity has been in determining mediums of acceptable payment. So let's take a nostalgic walk down money lane.

A BRIEF CHRONOLOGY OF MONEY

The barter system was the first method of payment, and it dates back to the beginning of time. To barter means to trade by exchanging one commodity for another. We learned very early in our existence that most other people would accept certain goods or services in exchange for their particular goods or services. These goods included, but were not limited to, animal hides, cloth, salt, and articles of gold or silver. The barter system is still in use today mainly because it is an effective form of determining value based upon the desires and value systems of the two parties involved, which is as valid today as it was centuries ago. It is also a useful form of exchange if currency becomes scarce or worthless, as is the case in some developing countries.

The first actual "money" appeared in the world in the form of cattle, that is, cows, sheep and camels. As agriculture became more widespread, agricultural products, especially grain, became currency, which was at its height in the period from about 9000 to 6000 B.C.

Around 1200 B.C., cowrie shells were introduced as a form of currency. Cowrie shells were the most widely used of any currency in history, and were in use for the longest period of time. Cowrie shells are the shells of a mollusk that was plentiful and easily harvested from warm seas such as the Pacific and Indian Oceans, and hence their popularity as currency. They are glossy and often brightly colored, adding to their value and attraction.

The first metal money appeared around 1000 B.C. in China at the end of the Stone Age. The coins were made of bronze or copper, and usually had holes in them so they could be strung together. Around 600 B.C., the first modern coins appeared. They were made out of lumps of silver and gold and were stamped with the images of various gods and rulers. These types of coins first appeared in Turkey, and were copied by the Greeks, Persians, Romans and Macedonians. Gold, silver and bronze were the most often used metals. Many historians believe that coins were also invented independently in ancient China and in India. In China, leather money was also being used around the same time. This consisted of foot long squares of white deerskin with colorful borders. Some consider these the first documented banknotes.

Between 600 and 800 A.D., the first real paper currency was placed in use, again in China. Other forms of currency still popped up in various places around the globe. For instance, in the 1500's, the Native Americans used wampum for currency, which consisted of strings of beads made from clamshells. The Europeans adopted paper money in the 1600's when banks began to issue paper bills, called bank notes. Until the 1800's, most of the paper bills in circulation were notes issued by banks or private companies rather than governments.

In 1816, the Gold Standard was officially adopted in England that set a standard of values for banking. In 1900, the United States Congress passed the Gold Standard Act that officially put the nation on a gold standard. The United States went on and off the gold standard several times over the years and the decision was made to finally eliminate it in 1971.

I took you through this abbreviated history of money to emphasize the point that money in and of itself is nothing, as it has taken many forms over the years. It has constantly evolved and continues to evolve. Money in the future may be of an entirely different form. We have already seen the rise of electronic money, and debit and credit cards. The one thing that stays constant, though, and the one thing that is really important is what money represents. But just what does money represent? When we talk about a medium of exchange to what are we referring? What is wealth and how do we measure it?

We live in a world of hidden meanings, of underlying significances, and so it follows that there must be a deeper meaning or significance to the idea of wealth and value. One way of getting closer to this underlying meaning is t look at what people do with money once they have it. If you took ten people off the street and gave them each a million dollars, they would probably all spend it in different ways. That is because money in and of itself is nothing until it is put into use. The use, then, is the real meaning or value of the money. And how do we determine how we will use money? By what money represents to us.

A look at why we want money will give us a clue as to what money really represents. There are many views of what money, wealth and prosperity represent to us, in other words, what its significance is to us, and we are now going to take a look at some of the most common ones. More than likely, you will find an idea or a view of money listed here that you either embrace currently or did at one point in your life. If, after reading through all of these uses and representations of money, you still aren't sure where you fit, ask yourself what you would do with a million dollars. Or another way of asking the question is, if money could buy happiness, what would you buy?

MONEY AS POWER

The first view we will tackle is that of money being the equivalent of power. This is the idea that if one is powerful, one has a lot of money. This view is quite prevalent today, and there are more believers than probably would actually admit it. After all, in ancient times, when the general won the war, he would pillage the town and take the gold and other valuables from his conquered lands for himself because that was his right. To be the conqueror meant that one had earned the right to control the wealth of the conquered land.

This same mindset is with us today, especially in world politics.

Governments with large amounts of money lend or give money to countries with very little money, and in return gain a certain amount of allegiance or loyalty from the country they aided. This is a form of power or control. Certainly, not all gifts from wealthy countries to less wealthy countries can be construed as simply issues of control; there can be true free giving without the expectation of anything in return. However, in the world forum, this is very rare, and usually aid is given with the expectation of receiving something in return, which then removes the gift from the charitable column to the control column.

This practice of giving with the expectation of receiving is acted out not only by countries but by individuals as well and I am sure we are all familiar with it. And this behavior is not limited to very wealthy people. It can occur in all economic walks of life. If you have ever given anyone anything with the idea of receiving something in return, or with the idea that your gift allows you control over some area of someone's life, then you are guilty as well. For instance, if you give your housekeeper an especially large bonus because you want to make sure that she does not leave you for another family, you are giving her the gift out of a desire to control her future activities. The only true gift is one freely given with no desire to receive anything in return. Since many of us equate power with money, this behavior is typical of many of us, whether we do it consciously or not.

From an astrological standpoint, the tendency to equate money with power or control speaks loudly of a Plutonian influence. If Pluto is strong in your chart and afflicts, or is in hard aspect to Venus, then the perversion of money for control or power is a possible outcome of the improper use of these energies. Also, any of the signs where power and control are important, for example, Leo, Capricorn, Aries, Scorpio and Taurus, and where this power is used for personal rather than humanitarian reasons, are also candidates for this particular view of money.

MONEY AS SECURITY

Our basic human needs, i.e., food, warmth, shelter, clothing, are all necessary to our survival and until they are taken care of, nothing else really matters. This is one of the main reasons that people hoard money. They are saving up for the inevitable rainy day. This makes sense on a certain level, albeit a very basic level, for if one is in tune with the universe, the desire for security is not as important. Being in tune with the universe would instill in an individual an element of trust that one's needs would always be met. But until we get to that point in our evolution, worry about fulfilling our basic needs can haunt us, and we can be driven to meet them.

Having the earth signs strong in one's chart could tend to give one this perspective of money. Also, an afflicted Moon could create this same preoccupation with basic survival instincts and thus to relate money to security. This is because the Moon adds a strong emotional element to the fulfilling of our basic needs, and we all know that adding emotion to anything makes it more important and in some cases, causes it to become the driving force in our existence.

Basic survival needs can be exaggerated to the point that they include things that aren't really basic needs at all, and that actually fall more into the category of wants and desires. A person can truly believe that these things are needs and that he cannot survive without them. Air conditioning, indoor toilets, phones, are these truly needs or just conveniences? The line is so blurred between needs and desires that it can sometimes take a lot of thought to recognize the difference.

MONEY AS LOVE

I buy things for myself to love myself. I buy things for others to show them how much I love them. The more I spend on them, the more I love them. This is the mantra of the person who sees money as representing love. Sometimes this is because the individual is narcissistic, but often it is because the person is lacking in confidence, and buying things for himself or others helps to create the image that he is loved. Or perhaps, we don't know how to attract love to ourselves, or how to show love to others, and so we buy things and try to fool ourselves into believing that we are very loving people.

Don't get me wrong. I am not saying that giving to others is bad. All I am saying here is that if the motive behind the giving is incorrect, then the giving takes on a different meaning. If we equate money with love, then we have bought into the belief that love can be purchased, or that material things represent love.

An afflicted Venus can sometimes cause this distortion, especially if Venus is in hard aspect to Pluto, which would add intensity to this already perverted view of love. Venus in Capricorn or Virgo, both very material signs, can also bring an element of materiality to the concept of love. Venus in hard aspect to Jupiter could create a self-indulgent type who would shower himself and others with material goods. In hard aspect to Neptune, we get the added dimension of self-delusion, and so someone could easily believe that they are truly in love or loved because of the material gifts they receive.

MONEY AS SOCIAL STATUS

I buy my friends. I have to have a certain amount of money to have the kinds of friends I want. Money buys friends and status. I can discriminate between who I want as my friends and who I don't. This mantra is not the same as money as power or money as love. This is the feeling that you want to be loved and adored by the world. You want to have a lot of friends. You want to be looked up to and admired. This is related to a very strong narcissistic view of life. You are the center and want the world to revolve around you, and the only way to do that is with lots of money. You are, to a certain degree, buying friends and social status.

The people with this attitude are those who have to have the largest house on the block, the most expensive car, and the trendiest clothes. These are the people who invented the saying, "it's not what you know but who you know." To these people, everything is about status and how you are viewed by others. This is keeping up with the Joneses taken to extremes.

This perverted view of status can be found with afflicted Saturns, since Saturn relates to worldly status. Also, planets in Capricorn or the tenth house, or Taurus and Virgo, making hard aspects especially to Venus, can create the idea of determining one's value based on one's possessions, or the caliber of one's friends.

MONEY AS VALIDATION

For some, money represents a pat on the back from society, the sign of a job well done. It is as if the world is saying to you that you have a very valuable gift to offer the world, and we thank you by giving you money for your services rendered. It is a sign that you did your job well. For others, money is a sign of a life well lived. They think that if they do everything right, they will be rewarded monetarily by the universe, and if they don't receive a monetary reward, then they have not lived their life correctly. This person wants money to give his life significance.

If we dig a little deeper, we will recognize that this outlook towards money relates to the way we value ourselves. We have set a definite value or price for our worth and if it is not met, then we believe our worth has not been recognized. This outlook towards money can also represent someone with very low self-esteem who is looking for money to raise his self-worth.

A person with a Leo Sun or Leo rising would be a likely candidate for this view of money, as would anyone who values himself or herself highly and looks for outward symbols of that value, such as someone with the Sun placed in the tenth house, or perhaps someone with Venus, the planet of values, in the first house, or someone with the second house of values prominent.

MONEY AS FREEDOM

Being able to do exactly what you want, when you want, or to do nothing at all, is extremely important to some, and so money represents the freedom to do just that. I am speaking here of personal freedom, not the more altruistic, humanitarian concept of freedom for all, i.e., freedom of religion, freedom of speech, etc. Those more altruistic ideas will be covered later. Right now, we are looking at the person who wants money because he doesn't want to have to go to work everyday. He wants to basically "buy his freedom" from the obligations of life.

You may want to be free to travel, or to write, or to sleep until noon everyday. Or, your list of personal freedoms may include more basic items such as freedom to choose where you will live or what you will eat, or what you will read. No matter the personal freedom, you are one who truly appreciates the view of money as freedom because it can buy that freedom for you.

Persons with Uranus powerful in their charts, or with many planets in Aquarius, will relate quite strongly to this classification of money. Also, those with Gemini or strong Mercurial energy in their charts don't like to be tied down either, so they also will appreciate this view of money. Sagittarian types and those with expansive Jupiter prominent in their charts are also prone to wandering and need plenty of personal freedom, so they would also be inclined to see money as the most logical way to obtain the personal freedom they desire.

The next two views of money are the best and the worst that money can represent. At some point, we all come to the realization that money as power, security, social status, validation, or freedom is just not enough. And so we reach the crossroads, and we decide either to become hoarders, those who never have enough money, or we become those who distribute money as a tool of goodwill.

MONEY FOR MONEY'S SAKE: THE HOARDER

At first glance, you may think that this is the same person as the one who sees money as representing security. However, with the hoarder, money is the goal itself. In other words, once the person has reached a very secure position in his life, he is still not satisfied. He wants money just for the sake of having it. You might be asking, isn't this the same as the person who wants money for power and control? Again, the answer is no. The person who wants power or control has an ultimate goal or use for the money. The hoarder has no use for the money. He just wants it. He will never use it, for good or bad. He just hoards it.

MONEY AS A TOOL OF GOODWILL

This person is the opposite of our hoarder, for this person sees money as a means to help others less fortunate, to spread goodwill on the planet, and to uplift humanity as a whole. For this person, money is not an end in itself, but only a tool to be used to accomplish humanitarian efforts. Of course, we all need money to live, and so a certain amount is necessary for our basic needs, but according to this view, any excess should be used to help others.

We have looked at all of these common views of money to help us see where we stand in relation to money. If you are struggling in your pursuit of money, it may be that you need to adjust your view of it in some way. The next chapter should be especially interesting because we are going to look at some ways of changing what money represents to us, and thus increase our chances of getting what we want.

But before we do that, let's go through each of the signs and see what money can mean to them, based on the categories outlined above. The sign descriptions are mainly for someone who has that particular Sun sign or rising sign, but it can also refer to anyone with a particular sign strong in their chart. For instance, if you have three or more planets in a certain sign, then you should read the description for that sign in addition to the paragraphs for your Sun and rising sign.

ARIES

Strong Aries types would be inclined to see money as a way of financing their projects. They are people of action, and are not afraid to show initiative. They listen to their inner voices and then go forward. They will often be found in the group that sees money as power, for it is the power to do whatever it is that they want to do. Those with strong Aries energy usually have natural leadership qualities, again relating to the idea of money as power or control. Additionally, these people may be inclined to see money as freedom, this time emphasizing the desire to be free to pursue one's goal without interference. As this sign can also indicate someone who is self-centered, a strong Aries type may also see money as a means of loving himself and putting himself first.

TAURUS

Since Taurus is the first of the earth signs, security and having a solid foundation would be quite important to them. Money is a means of achieving both of these things, and so money representing security would probably be number one. Carried to extremes, those with an enormous amount of Taurean energy may even fall into the hoarder category, simply because this person may have so many material desires that money is hoarded in order to insure that there is always enough.

GEMINI

Those individuals born with a lot of Gemini energy in their charts are a very independent lot, and so being tied down is something they dread; that's one reason they keep moving. It is very typical, then, for this type of person to see money as representing freedom, the freedom to keep moving, the freedom to have many relationships, and many experiences. This is part of the all-consuming learning process so important to Gemini types, as money allows for the easy pursuit of knowledge.

CANCER

Cancerian energy is strongly tied to the home, family and foundation, and therefore, this is one of the main signs that would be inclined to view money as security and also as love. As in the case of Taurus, if this desire for security is carried to extremes, it can lead to hoarding. This energy, at its lowest, is notorious for holding tightly onto material things in an attempt to guarantee security. They continually save up for that rainy day, and at some point, may have difficulty in determining how much is enough.

LEO

Those strong in Leo energy usually have a highly developed sense of self, and so they are will aware of their own worth, and as a result, are typical of those who view money as validation, as a public recognition of their worth or value to society. Related to this would be the view of money as social status, or money as love. There can be a tendency in those with a lot of Leo energy in their charts, to see themselves as the center of their little universe, and thus deserving of large amounts of love, adoration and fulfillment of personal desires, and money can be used to promote one's social status or standing in the community, as well as to shower oneself with gifts. Also, this is a sign that likes to wield power over others, so money as power or control is also likely here.

VIRGO

As an earth sign, security issues are quite strong, so it is very common for those with a lot of Virgo energy to view money as security. And just like Taurus and Cancer, those with a lot of Virgo energy can easily fall into the hoarder category if they carry their quest for security to extremes. They can also be extremely status conscious, due to their highly discriminating nature. Therefore, money as status could be another of their views. This energy is also related to the hard-working, service-oriented person, so money may also be viewed as validation of one's worth or the value of one's service.

LIBRA

Librans are mental types, so possible views of money would be money as freedom to pursue mental pursuits, or money as validation for their mental prowess. But most likely, those with a lot of Libran energy, due to their love of beauty and harmony, will see money as the equivalent of love, or money as social status. They would be inclined to see money as the tool to beautify their surroundings, as a way of loving themselves, or of showering their family and friends with beautiful things, again as a way of showing love. Additionally, using money to surround themselves with harmonious or "beautiful" people could be the manifestation of money as social status.

SCORPIO

Scorpionic energy can give one a tendency towards an emotional view of money, most closely associated with the categories of money as security and money as love. However, the most probable view of money held by someone with a lot of Scorpio energy in his or her chart would be to view money as power. This is definitely one of the signs that like to wield power and control, and so using money for strategic purposes, to gain favors, etc., would definitely appeal to many of these types.

SAGITTARIUS

These individuals are the most optimistic of the zodiac, so money as security would probably not be a common view. Money as love, though, may be prominent in some types. Money as freedom, however, is the most likely view to be held, as Sagittarian types are known for their love of travel. They don't want to be pinned down to one spot; having a lot of money would allow them to travel as often as they would like, to see the world and to meet and learn from as many people as possible.

CAPRICORN

This can be one of the most materialistic of all the signs, and so money as security would certainly be important to many with strong Capricorn energy in their charts. Those with a lot of Capricorn energy can lean toward negativity and so wanting to hoard money because of fear of the worst is also possible. This is also a sign of power and so money as power and control would also rank high in the view of many of these people. Additionally, Capricorns are achievement oriented, so money as social status as well as money as validation could be quite important.

AQUARIUS

Those with strong Aquarian energies are very likely to view money as freedom. They want freedom of movement, to be able to do whatever they want, and to express themselves in a free and open way. For many Aquarians, a belief that money would allow them that freedom is quite strong. Also, this is a mental sign, therefore freedom to pursue intellectual activities would be important as well.

PISCES

Pretty much all of the categories representing money could show up here, as Pisces is the composite of all of the signs of the zodiac. Money as social status and money as power would probably not be as common, since Pisceans are noted for their compassion, but there are a few Pisceans that can muster the necessary grounding (after all, Virgo, an earth sign, is their opposite) to put security high up on their list. And since this is a water sign, the emotional money as security category could also be a popularly held view. Money as love, though, would probably top the list.

Highly evolved persons of all signs would, to some degree, view money as a tool of goodwill, and so even though this category was not mentioned in the above review of the signs, if you are one of those who see the purpose of money as an instrument to help others, then you are well on your way towards a very enlightened attitude regarding money.

Next, we will take a look at planetary energies and how they relate to one's perception of money. Again, when considering these energies, you need to examine your natal chart and see which planets exert the most influence. Any planet that is angular, i.e., a planet in the first, fourth, seventh, or tenth house, is extremely important, as is the planet which rules your Sun sign and Ascendant. A planet that aspects the Ascendant, Descendant, Midheaven or Nadir or your Sun or Moon would also be considered to be strong in your chart.

SUN

The Sun is important in any chart, but if it is angular, or in aspect to the angles, then you are a very lucky person indeed. The Sun will shed a large amount of light in the area in which it resides, and so it follows that light would be shed on or highlight your particular view of money and what it represents to you. This view of money can either highlight you or it can highlight others or a higher cause. If it highlights you, then the most likely view of money would be that of love, self-love, and love of those close to you. If it highlights others or a higher cause, then you may see someone who views money as a tool of goodwill. Those with the Sun prominent who see themselves as the center of their own personal universes may also embrace the view of money as power or control, or money as validation. However, those more advanced people who have learned to use the warmth and generosity of the Sun for the benefit of others may view money as a tool of goodwill.

MOON

The Moon relates to our past, to our ingrained behaviors, and to our emotional responses. It is our base, and is imminently related to our security. If the Moon is strong in your chart, you instinctively view money as security and proceed through life unconsciously gathering everything that you need to feel secure. This is the energy that gives us the greatest tendency to hoard money, for the subconscious pull for security can be very strong, and you may not even be aware of how powerful the effect is. If you are able to extricate yourself from this powerful pull, you may discover that your priorities will shift, and as a result, your views about money will shift also. It is possible to overcome those ingrained, emotional responses, and respond to a higher energy, one that is less security driven and more humanity driven.

MERCURY

This is the mental planet, the communicator, the messenger of the gods, and the bridge between the higher and lower minds. Those with strong Mercurial influences are continually gathering information, distilling it, and then dispersing it. As a result, their view of money may constantly change, based on the amount and quality of information they have collected on the subject. Since "air" or the freedom to circulate as freely as the air is quite important to those with a lot of Mercurial energy, the view of money as freedom would be very prevalent. However, it is conceivable that a large amount of Mercurial energy may also give one the tendency to view money as goodwill if they are more connected to the higher rather than the lower mind.

VENUS

An abundance of Venusian energy implies a highly developed capacity to love, or at least a highly developed sense of beauty and art, and an appreciation of the finer things in life. The question is whether or not this love is of a personal or impersonal nature. If it is more of a personal nature, expect that the person would be inclined to view money as love, or money as status, as in both cases, money would be used to lavish oneself with the best, the most beautiful and the most expensive. Taken up a notch, a person with a strong Venus is their chart who has learned to see the wisdom side of love, that is, to love impersonally, would also be capable of seeing, through this combination of intelligence and love, that money can be viewed as a tool of goodwill to show love for all instead of using it to show love for himself only.

MARS

This is the planet that represents energy and strong desire, and anyone with Mars strong in their chart would relentlessly pursue their goals. Money to this type of person would more than likely represent power, the power to achieve their desired end. They may also view money as freedom, the freedom to pursue their goals uninhibited. Finally, depending on the nature of the goals or desires, if the goals are high enough, these people may also view money as a tool for goodwill and use their money and energy to achieve altruistic goals.

JUPITER

Since this is the planet of benevolence, those with strong Jupiterian energies would probably have an innate understanding of the bounty of the universe, and thus would not be so driven to acquire money for security, unless they were of very low character. Since they don't worry so much about security, they are usually well taken care of by the universe. An inner belief in the goodness of the universe often manifests as generosity towards others, and so this person could also be one of those who view money as a tool of goodwill. The expansiveness of Jupiter could also relate to the idea of limitlessness, and so money as freedom may also be prevalent.

SATURN

Saturn restricts, disciplines, and doles out karmic responsibilities, rewards, and opportunities. A strong Saturnian type would therefore be very sober and responsible in his or her views towards money. This serious, responsible approach to money would more than likely result in someone who took the view of money as security being basic and of utmost importance. This person would approach the subject of security in a responsible, straightforward fashion, for they understand all too well the negative consequences of failure. Someone with a strong Saturn may be inclined to feel that their life is very karmic, or that there are many debts that need to be repaid, therefore, if one is at all inclined towards a higher view of money, this person may view money as goodwill as a karmic responsibility.

URANUS

Strong Uranian types fall into two categories, those who are different for different's sake, and those who are truly original and ahead of their time. Either one would have revolutionary views on all issues, including the meaning of money, and so they would be inclined either to view money in the most revolutionary way, that of money existing solely for the purpose of goodwill, or they would take the more personal view, giving them the opportunity to express their uniqueness to the world which in our study, represents money as freedom.

NEPTUNE

Neptune represents the higher octave of Venus, and so someone with strong Neptunian energy can be attuned to a higher, more idealistic vision of money and how it is to be used. This is not always the case, but it is very possible. There can be, however, a lot of unclear and distorted views regarding money with this placement, as Neptune can cast a large cloud of fog over one's thinking processes. If one is walking around in a "fog," one's perceptions may be totally unrealistic, and therefore, one's view of money may be any of the common views we discussed above, depending on other indications in the chart.

PLUTO

Pluto has to do with intensity and personal power, so anyone with a lot of Plutonian energy in their chart has a strong connection to power and control issues. This can be either good or bad, depending on how the energy is used. If the tendency is toward controlling others and bending them to your will, then the tendency to view money as a means to achieve this control will usually be prevalent. Pluto also has to do with death and transformation, and so transformation of the personality, and thus the personality's views of money, is quite possible. Therefore, someone with Pluto strong in the chart may change, or transform his or her view of money and of what it represents over the course of a lifetime. This person may eliminate all of his incorrectly held views of money and could learn to see money in a different, more universal light.

CHAPTER 7

CHASING THE GOAL INSTEAD OF THE MONEY

In this chapter, we're going to try an experiment. This experiment may seem a little silly at first, but please give it a chance before dismissing it. This experiment has to do with substituting one idea for another, with the goal of proving that both ideas are the equivalent of each other. In order to clarify the experiment, I would like you to think back to our ten hypothetical people in the last chapter who were each given a million dollars. We hypothesized that the money would be spent differently by each of the ten people because the money would have a different meaning for each person. And so, from this hypothesis, we deduced that the value of money really is what it represents to that particular person, not the money itself. And if that is the case, then it would follow that if we pursued what money represented instead of the money itself, then we would arrive at the same place. Right?

That is what this experiment is all about. We are going to look at ways of pursuing the goal instead of the money and see if we end up in the same place. We will have to be very creative, for this is an unstructured experiment and we are venturing into uncharted territory. We must also be open minded, as this is also a mental pursuit, and like a scientist, we must look at all the possibilities and not make any hasty decisions until we have weighed all the facts.

The concept of pursuing the goal instead of the money may be too simple an idea to many of you, and to a certain degree, you are right. It is a simple idea, but the most basic truths in life are simple. They are so simple that they have become clichés and we ignore them because we have heard them so many times. Do unto others, honesty is the best policy, etc., have been quoted so often that the true meaning has become lost. Being the thinking beings that we are, we cannot accept the idea that the key to a successful life can be that simple, and so we come up with complicated theories that, in turn, complicate our lives, and then we lament the fact that we can't seem to find our way through life. Our necessarily complicated lives lead to stress which leads to nervous breakdowns, hair loss, lack of sleep and innumerable other negative effects. We live lives of pain, physical, emotional and mental, and we don't know how to fix them. One of the most popular sayings of the time is, "Life sucks and then you die." Well, I believe just the opposite, that life is beautiful, and we just need to simplify.

My simplification process is going to start with our view of money. Money has caused a lot of unhappiness because people don't understand what it really means. Too many of us equate money with happiness. We complain that we don't have enough money to be happy, and yet, that old cliché says that money doesn't buy happiness. But we don't believe it because we have seen wealthy people who look happy to us and so we conclude that it must be that money does buy happiness. Our experiment is going to propose the hypothesis that it isn't the money that brings the happiness, but the use of the money, the goal. Secondly, by pursuing the goal instead of the money, our lives will be simpler, less stressful, and a lot happier.

Now, we need to set up some ground rules for our experiment. Establishing parameters will keep us from straying too far off track. We already talked about approaching this experiment, first of all, with an open mind, and secondly, with imagination and creativity. Those, then, are our first two rules. Ground rule number three has to do with eliminating certain preconceived notions. Going back to simple rules, we have heard many times that we ought to pursue what makes us happy, and the money will follow. This a simple rule that I want to tweak just a little bit. If we do what makes us happy to earn a living, we will in many instances, learn to hate the thing that we once loved, for once we equate it to money, it loses the quality that made it fun. The reason that it was fun was because it was something we enjoyed doing that we didn't have to do to earn money. So, ground rule number three is this: Figure out what money represents to you and separate the goal from the fun activity.

Let me give you an example of what I mean. Writing for me is fun. I write because I like to do it. I have three planets in Gemini, including Mercury, and so I like to write. I write and I don't care if I make any money from it at all. I write because it is therapeutic. I write because I feel I know some things that may help other people and I write about them because I like it. If I am fortunate enough to be able to publish a book I have written, that is wonderful because I would love for my books to help other people. But even if I never published a single book, I would still write. I don't write books for the money. If I wrote books just to make money, I would not like writing anymore and I would probably be very disappointed. If I wrote books to make money, I wouldn't necessarily write what I liked or what would help other people; I would simply write what I thought would sell. One of my goals or views of money is freedom, freedom to write what I want and freedom to share my knowledge and ideas with others. Freedom is the goal and writing is a way for me to achieve that goal.

Here's another example. Suppose money represents security to you. Suppose you also love to cook. Now, many people will tell you that you should open a catering business or perhaps a restaurant, and you would have the perfect career. To meet the parameters of this experiment, though, you would want to make sure that you do not equate cooking with money and/or security. The quest for security should be your guiding light. Go after the house or whatever it is that represents security to you and leave your happy hobby safely locked way in another area of your brain so that you don't contaminate it. You can still make money from your cooking, but do not cook to make money. Cook because you love it. If you happen to receive money for doing something you love, that's fine. But if you don't receive any money from it, that's okay too because you never really expected to. You expect to have security and to pursue that, you pursue security-minded activities, such as learning how to invest any monies that you do receive for maximum growth, taking financial planning classes, etc. Security is the goal, not cooking.

So let's review our three ground rules. Number one is to keep an open mind, that is, take a scientific approach to our experiment. Number two is to use our imagination and creativity. Number three is to make sure that we don't substitute our hobby for our goal. With those three rules understood, it is now time to move forward and start the actual experiment. We begin by looking at the categories of what money represents to us that we discussed in the last chapter, only this time, we will look at them as the goal in and of itself instead of merely as a representation of money. We will try to identify ways to achieve the particular goal without bringing money into the picture. We will observe and take notes like a good scientist, and at the end of the chapter, we will draw our conclusions.

MONEY AS POWER

How do you use your quest for power as a goal? Prove to the world that you are a leader. Leaders have power and control over others. One way to accomplish this would be to assume leadership roles whenever and wherever they are offered to you. No leadership role is too small, for it can be good practice and may lead to other, more important leadership positions. Whenever possible, take the lead. When you are with a group of people, for instance, always walk in front and make the others follow you. Another way to show your leadership talents would be through volunteering, and then finding ways to showcase your organizational and administrative skills. Be the decision maker. Make your reputation as the one who steps forward in times of crisis and calmly delegates duties. Let others see that you possess these skills, and you will find that you are called upon time after time to be the leader. Eventually, people will automatically think of you as the one in control, the one in power, anytime a crisis arrives or a decision has to be made.

One thing that true leaders and those in control always possess is a loyal following, or at least one very loyal friend. The Long Ranger had Tonto, Luke Skywalker had Chewbaca, and all real kings have a kingdom of loyal subjects. King Arthur had his knights of the round table, all having sworn allegiance to him. Cultivate this ability to attract loyal followers. Learn to develop your own entourage. This is the true sign of someone in power: the fact that others look up to you. The best way to make others look up to you is to show leadership. It is a dynamic circle, and one that works.

MONEY AS SECURITY

How do you pursue security instead of money? It's a mindset.

You perceive everything that comes into your life from the point of view of your future security and how it can help you in pursuit of that goal. You make decisions based on security. You read financial journals, attend financial planning seminars, make a will and an estate plan, and develop an investment strategy. You seek advice from those who are already "secure" according to your personal definition of the word. You watch them and you imitate them.

On a more mundane level, you learn to always ask, "What if?" and then set out to prepare yourself for every possible contingency. As a security conscious person, you consistently look for bargains. You embrace in the depths of your soul the admonition to buy low and sell high. You shop only at sales, never paying retail for anything. You buy in bulk, so that you never run out of staples. You drive your car for ten years instead of getting anew one every season.

If security is your goal, you always want to make sure that you have enough of everything so that you never go wanting. Being frugal is the most consistent way to achieve this; you learn to wisely use what you have. You learn to stretch a budget and get by on less. This is a very unromantic way to approach life, and yet it very practical and will ultimately yield the security you desire, at least up to a point. There are certain contingencies that we just cannot anticipate and thus cannot totally prepare for, such as wars and natural disasters, but we can be as prepared as is reasonably possible for such events, which is all a human could hope for.

MONEY AS LOVE

This is a fairly easy goal compared to the earlier ones. If money represents love to you, and you want to pursue that goal, then love yourself and those around you. And how do you do this? You love yourself by making sure that you always put yourself and your needs first. This may sound selfish, but not if you remember that the goal here is about the self. To love the self is not always all bad. To treat yourself kindly by doing all the little things that give you joy can actually help you to get to know who you really are, your true inner self, and will allow you then to work on those traits and skills that are worth developing, and to eliminate the negative ones. Carrying this one step further, it allows you to then foster an appreciation of your talents and abilities, which is essential for proper growth and fulfillment and helps to insure that you will eventually find your way to your proper career.

The way to love yourself, then, is to spoil yourself. Allow yourself to eat all your favorite treats, buy that special article of clothing, or attend the play that you have been dying to see. Give yourself whatever you need to make yourself feel pampered and special. Shower those you love with the same kind of treatment. Your children, who are your greatest treasures, are especially deserving of your attentions and kindnesses. You want to show them that you love them also, and in turn, foster in them a self-love. By loving yourself, you are showing the world that you value yourself and your loved ones. Sending out that message will, in turn, attract people with similar values and people who truly value you for who you are. You can be confident that their love is sincere because they know the real you, your true self which you have clearly defined and presented so magnificently to the world.

MONEY AS SOCIAL STATUS

Pursuing the goal of social status starts from within. It is an attitude that permeates your consciousness and affects your every action. Social status is defined differently by each of us. But once you have finally determined your definition of status, then you can go after it. For instance, if you definition of social status means having the right friends and being in the right crowd, then pursue that with a vengeance. If you define social status as having the right clothes or the right car, then that must be your goal. Social status doesn't have to start with a lot of money. Status is determined by what others think of you, and that has more to do with perception than anything else.

If you can make others think that you have something better than they have, then you have achieved social status. You do this by determining what others in your group think is important, and then securing it for yourself. Every social group, no matter what the economic status, has certain beliefs, rituals, and core values. Status in the eyes of the group is based upon these beliefs and values. Figuring out the core values of your group will allow you to know how to gain status in their eyes.

MONEY AS VALIDATION

Closely related to social status is validation because this view of money is also tied to how you are perceived by others. The difference this time is that you want others to appreciate you for something you have done. You want public recognition for having performed your job well, for having succeeded at some important task, or for anything you feel you have accomplished that deserves recognition, including a life well lived. You want this recognition or acknowledgement because it will make you feel valued, loved and validated by others.

To pursue this as your goal, the first thing you need to do is clearly define what it is that you want to be acknowledged for having accomplished. Implicit in this goal is the fact that you have actually accomplished something worthy of note. Once you have identified your accomplishment, the next step is to let others know about it, especially those whose acceptance you crave. If you want to be acknowledged, you must become your own publicist. You have to find ways of getting the message out. Telling people who you know will talk is a good place to start. Keeping yourself in the public eye is another route. Never pass up an opportunity to let others know what you have been doing. This is no time for modesty or humility. Speak up and let others know of your accomplishments and what you are capable of accomplishing in the future. Eventually, not only will you be acknowledged, but you will also find that you are often called upon to do other, more important things because you have made it known that you are competent. This in turn will bring future acknowledgement and validation. It is a beautifully vicious circle.

MONEY AS FREEDOM

Freedom implies that there is nothing holding you or forcing you to stay in a situation in which you don't want to be. By situation, I am referring to a place, a relationship, a career, job or position, or anything else that you could at some time consider confining. Therefore, if you are to pursue the goal of freedom, do not allow any situation to become confining.

Pursuing this goal requires quite a bit of instinct and intuition, for you will have to be able to very quickly recognize when a situation is beginning to change from comfortable to confining. It is of the utmost importance that you acknowledge an uncomfortable position right away, for the longer you stay in a confining situation, the harder it is to extricate yourself. So, you must always be on your guard. You must never see yourself as being in one place for too long. Permanent is a word that is not in your vocabulary.

You want a life with no boundaries, no limits. On all levels of life, then, from the mental to the emotional to the physical, you want to lessen your load because you want to be able to move into a new situation at the drop of a hat. Therefore, on the physical level, you should try to always travel light. You don't need to own too many things, for they will just weigh you down. On the mental level, this means that you cannot allow yourself to become limited or provincial in your thinking. And finally, you must allow yourself to remain open to all kinds of experiences on the emotional level. As with all the goals we have discussed so far, freedom is a state of mind, and by developing that state of mind, you will soon see that you will attract all of the attributes and benefits that go along with it.

MONEY FOR MONEY'S SAKE: THE HOARDER

Unfortunately, this is one view that is beyond the idea of chasing the goal instead of the money, for the hoarder sees money, and only money, as the goal. Therefore, anyone in this position has to first ease himself back into one of the previous six representations of money and then work from there. The way to do that would be to ask yourself how you because a hoarder in the first place. Did you perhaps start out wanting money for security and then get carried away? Were you initially interested in money for status and then somehow became so caught up in the idea that you slipped into the hoarding category? You need to take a look at each of the categories and ask yourself these questions until you can figure out which fits you the best. Hoarding is the pursuit of money in the extreme, and can be overcome if you are honest with yourself as you go through this process.

Sometimes it is difficult to get to the root of the matter, for there can be many factors clouding the truth, and you will have to figure out how to get rid of the things that don't have any relation to the real issue. If you are having trouble, you might ask yourself what kinds of things you buy when you do spend money. See if the nature of the purchases will all fit into one of the previous categories, i.e., power, security, etc. If they fall all over the place, ask yourself what you would keep if you had to return everything except one item. This exercise may take a little time, but once you have found your root relationship to money, it is simply a matter of following the instructions given for the appropriate category.

MONEY AS A TOOL OF GOODWILL

This is the other monetary extreme, but at the positive end of the scale. If you are in this category, that is, if your view of money and therefore your goal is to do good for others, then it is just a matter of doing those things that will make this goal become a reality. For instance, you may have envisioned opening a school in an under-developed country, or perhaps a hospital in a rural area. Or perhaps something on a smaller scale, like sponsoring a child through World Vision, or buying uniforms for a low income area children's baseball team. Maybe you want to mentor a child, or help establish low cost childcare in your neighborhood. There are any number of possibilities, and since this is your goal, it will be much better than anything I could list here because it is your vision, not mine. The most important thing is that you start to do something about it.

Next, let's go through each of the signs and planets and see how those energies can be used to help us in the pursuit of our new mindset, that is, chasing the goal instead of the money. A sign is strong in your chart if your Sun or any of the angles are placed there, in particular the Ascendant. Also, if you have several planets in a particular sign, that energy would be strong in your chart as well.

ARIES

Pursuing the goal instead of the money should actually be quite easy for an Aries type. After all, they are always the first ones out of the gate of life, and it is usually because they have a goal or agenda already in mind. Noted for their courage, they are also normally driven in the pursuit of their goal, at least initially. People with a lot of Aries energy are very good at listening to their inner voice, so all it would take for an Aries person to adopt this mindset is to use their vast stores of courage to follow their intuition.

TAURUS

Taurus energy can be used as a solid and practical approach to achieving their goal. Anyone with a lot of Taurus energy in their chart would be quite good at attracting what they want, due to Taurus' link to the planet Venus. Therefore, you can call upon this magnetic energy to help you make the goal become a reality. Taurus does this through the use of strong desires. They instinctively know how to use desire to help them achieve what they want. So if you are blessed with a lot of Taurus energy and you want, or desire, the goal enough, you can focus that desire and your ample perseverance to help you attract it.

GEMINI

Those with a lot of Gemini energy in their horoscopes should be able to approach any goal from a completely mental perspective. As a Gemini individual, you will be able to think clearly, and more importantly, you will be able to clearly articulate the goal. Being able to identify the goal is the first step in being able to pursue it. You should also be good at strategizing, for you can mentally and systematically outline the steps required to achieve your goal.

CANCER

This is a nurturing, mothering kind of energy. Its best use is to make others feel safe, secure and protected. The best way to use this energy in pursuit of your goal is to nurture or mother your goal. You can view your goal as your child, if you want, and treat it as such. As your child, you would take care of it by giving it food, shelter and love. You would protect it from the outside world, and from cruel and mean forces that would try to hurt or destroy it. If Cancer is strong in your chart, you can use this energy to keep your goal safe and protected until it is able to stand on its own. In addition to your mothering qualities, you are also extremely sensitive, therefore you can feel or sense what needs to be done to keep you and your goal on track.

LEO

This is the energy of the lion, i.e., courage with a big heart. So much can be done to pursue your goal if you are strong in Leo traits and energy, for you have a powerful, innate belief in your own worth and abilities. The natural leadership qualities that this sign bestows can be used to masterfully guide your goal to fruition. You are the big picture person, and you know how to delegate. You are able to find the best-qualified people to work with you, under your direction, of course, to achieve the goal, and they work hard for you because you also know how to gain their respect as a magnanimous and generous leader. This energy is ideal for achieving a large goal, for Leo types works very well as the leader of a large group of people united in a common undertaking.

VIRGO

Virgos are known for their ability to discriminate, and so this quality can be used quite effectively to not only eliminate unrealistic or unattainable goals, but also to pick and choose the correct method of operation, and the correct people to be involved with the goal. Those strong in Virgo energy also possess a natural ability to give things form, due to the fact that this is an earth sign, and also because they are so good with details. Virgo types know exactly what needs to be done to make something happen, and they are able to perform those duties with accuracy and precision. Any goal left in their hands will be brought painstakingly and skillfully to fruition.

LIBRA

Libran energy is about balance, about being able to see the benefits of both sides and then reaching a suitable compromise. This harmonizing ability can be used to identify the pros and cons all along the way in pursuit of a particular goal, and by seeing both sides of any issue, you can then choose the middle course, insuring that the project will stay afloat. Going from one extreme to the other can be very damaging to a goal, as extremism can cause the entire goal to be lost or destroyed. Therefore, Libran energy is very valuable where sensitive negotiations are called for, because you are able to very carefully avoid a lot of mistakes through diplomatic handling of situations where other signs with less diplomatic tendencies might fail. Implicit in this sign is the idea of fairness or justice, and this is another trait you bring to your dealings with others in pursuit of your goal.

SCORPIO

This energy is excellent for strategic planning. Although Scorpionic energy is best described as emotional, it is quite powerful, and can be used to energize the project or goal towards which you are working with passion and a do or die attitude. An abundance of Scorpio energy brings great resourcefulness, thus you will be able to find a way to succeed, no matter what. If achieving your goal requires staying power, this is the energy to call upon. Scorpio is the sign of death as well, and that could be death to many things including personality traits or erroneous or outdated ideas. A strong Scorpio influence could be used, then, to "kill" any incorrect assumptions standing in the way of achieving your goal.

SAGITTARIUS

With a strong Sagittarius influence, you are able to see exactly where you are going and are able to follow the goal or vision to its end. The symbol of this sign, the arrow, is indicative of this innate or intuitive ability of Sagittarian natives to always know where they are going, and so they are very capable of leading others. If you feel yourself getting lost, call upon the Sagittarius energy in your chart to help get you back on the right path. Not only can it help you see clearly, but it can also help you attract others who can assist you by following your lead. Sagittarian energy is also beneficial in maintaining balance. It can be used to ensure that you are on solid ground before going on to the next step, thus avoiding pitfalls or having to retrace your steps.

CAPRICORN

Capricorn types are usually always pursuing a goal, so this energy is perfect for our experiment. If you have a lot of Capricorn in your chart, more than likely you are quite achievement oriented and already understand the steps involved in the process of defining and achieving a goal. But just in case you are not, here is a quick course in Capricorn goal-achieving strategies. First of all, they believe in slow, steady plodding towards the goal, and definitely no short cuts allowed. These people understand intuitively that you have to earn your rewards in life; nothing is free. And they are quite willing to expend the effort, for they know that the rewards are worthwhile. Capricorn energy also brings a lot of perspective to the individual so that wise choices can be made, another valuable asset in achieving any goal.

AQUARIUS

Aquarian energy is wonderful because it gives you an impersonal and mental approach towards the achievement of your goal. By removing all emotionalism from the equation, Aquarius energy allows you to assess problems in a matter of fact way, so that the objectives remain clear. You know intuitively exactly why your goal exists in the form that it does, and its ultimate purpose. Not only that, if you have a lot of Aquarian energy in your chart, you tend to think in a broad manner and are therefore not afraid to consider new and unorthodox methods for achieving your goal. This is a valuable trait if you find yourself stuck and unable to figure out how to proceed. You can very easily think outside the box.

PISCES

Finally, if you have a lot of Piscean energy in your chart, you are quite versatile in the pursuit of your goal. You can "go with the flow." Piscean types can very easily compromise if compromise is called for, but they can just as easily hold their own if they intuitively know that the situation calls for a tough stance. They patiently work their way towards their goal. The best time to call in your Piscean power is when things look insurmountable and you feel like giving up. This energy will allow you to visualize the best possible outcome, and it will also give you a sense of peace and faith that you will eventually reach your goal.

Now that we have looked at what each of the signs has to offer in the pursuit of our goal, we will do this same exercise with planetary energies. If a planet is strong in your chart, it should be well placed or aspected. By that I mean that it should be angular or it should be aspecting the Sun or an angle, particularly the Ascendant.

SUN

The Sun highlights or shines light upon the areas it touches in our charts. If the Sun is strong in your chart, its energies can be used to help you clearly see and focus attention upon your goal. The Sun warms things up, and can bring a very personal and intimate quality to everyone and everything close to you. So whatever your goal is, the energies of the Sun will make it shine. You can use your Sun to bring emphasis to your cause or to showcase your talents. A strong Sun is particularly helpful if your goal is validation, for it will not only bring attention to you, but it will help you in almost any endeavor. If yours is a goal that requires a lot of assistance from others, this energy can help you convince others to come to your aid, for it puts you and your goal in the best possible light.

MOON

The Moon brings a very strong emotional element, and so any goal requiring an extra large dose of emotional desire would be well served a strong Moon. If the goal is love, for instance, there would a lot of emotion invested in its pursuit, which would make one more likely to achieve it. But really, a large emotional investment should be beneficial in almost every endeavor. The only thing to watch out for is that you don't become so emotionally involved that you act irrationally. Also, a strong Moon may make you resistant to newer or more innovative ways of pursuing your goal, so watch out for this tendency also. Use your strong Moon to envelope your goal with the support, desire and love to support it until it is ready to be released.

MERCURY

This planet brings in the mental element, and so you can use these energies to plan and strategize the best way to achieve your goal. If Mercury is powerful in your chart, you will not have a shortage of ideas as to how to proceed and you will also be blessed with the ability to sift through these ideas and find the one that is the most appropriate. When a rational analysis needs to be made, Mercury can be depended upon to assist you in that regard. Also, Mercurial energy allows you to keep making progress. There is no stagnation where this planet is involved, for it is constantly moving from place to place. If you are focused on your goal, this movement can help keep your project advancing along at a swift pace. If you have a strong Mercury, you need to be careful of one thing. Do not be in too big of a hurry to move on to the next step until you are sure that you have adequately completed the previous one.

VENUS

A well-placed Venus allows you to see and comprchend what it is that you truly value. Knowing what you value can then help you to determine whether or not your goal is in line with your values. This is an important factor, for if your goal is inconsistent with your values, you most likely will not see it through to fruition. So if Venus is strong in your chart, the first thing to do in this exercise is to examine your goal from the perspective of values. Ask yourself if it is what you truly want, and if the answer is yes, then proceed. Otherwise, rethink your goal, which means going back to your original concept or representation of money. The other important function of Venus in our exercise is that of magnetism. A powerful Venus will allow you to draw your strongest desires to yourself, so it is very important that these desires pass the initial test of being in line with your true values.

MARS

Martian energies are those of the warrior. When you know your goal, a strong Mars in your chart will give you the strength to fight for it to the death. Mars is all about energy, physical strength and vitality, so no matter what the goal, you will be driven to pursue it and will have the stamina to do so. Mars is also related to intense desires, and so this intensity of emotion can be applied to your goal to help in making it a reality. You can also call upon your Martian power to give you the courage to stand tall when you are facing difficulties or formidable adversaries. Courage can mean the difference between seeing a project through to completion, or giving up.

JUPITER

Jupiter provides the optimism and fortuitous luck that allows you to achieve your goals without seemingly any effort on your part. If Jupiter is strong in your chart, then you will have the ability to see the possibilities of your goal long before you have achieved it. Jupiter, because of its expansive tendencies, allows you to expand your vision. Anyone with a strong Jupiter is very blessed. It is as if you have a guardian angel with you all the time, making sure that your wishes are granted, and that you don't have to endure any hardships in the area it is guarding. If you have a powerful Jupiter, you understand intuitively how a positive attitude and optimism can help bring a goal to fruition.

SATURN

You may think that because of Saturn's seriousness and hardness, this energy would not be very helpful in our experiment. However, you would be very mistaken. Saturnian energy is exactly what is needed in order to manifest anything, whether it is a goal or money. So, if we want to manifest our goal, the more that Saturn is involved, the better, for Saturn gives everything form. A powerful Saturn in your chart will give you the patience, determination and serious attitude necessary to persevere, and perseverance is one of the basic keys necessary to open the door of success. A strong Saturn can also be called upon to give you the focus to block out all distractions and to eliminate all roadblocks.

URANUS

Uranus adds its own unique brand of excitement to whatever area of your life it touches, and so a powerful Uranus will give you the ability to see the world from this new and exciting perspective. This excitement can be carried over to your goal, and can show itself in the form of enthusiasm, originality and creativity. Since Uranus is the planet of originality, with its help, you can approach your goal in a revolutionary way, either by taking an old approach and updating it, or simply throwing out all the old ideas and starting with fresh ones. Use a powerful Uranus to help you arrive at the highest and best possible version of your goal by thinking creatively and imaginatively.

NEPTUNE

If Neptune is strong in your chart, you can use that energy to help you idealize your goal and also to see how you should be pursuing it if it is to realize its greatest potential. Neptune will showcase your goal in the best possible light, allowing you and others to envision a perfect outcome. Use your Neptunian energy to uplift yourself and others by bringing in higher thoughts, ideas and purposes. A strong Neptune can also be used to encourage an emotional investment in your goal. We discussed earlier how a strong emotional investment could help ensure that the goal is achieved. Also, Neptune, as the higher octave of Venus, will bring strong magnetic qualities, again aiding in the manifestation process.

PLUTO

Pluto brings intensity to the area of your life it touches. If you are strong on Pluto qualities, you are very intense and have a larger than normal amount of stamina and staying power. Pluto, like Mars, bestows inner strength, only this strength seems to go on forever, drawn from a well deep within you. This energy can be focused and channeled toward the achievement of your goal, and it also goes a long way towards ensuring success simply because you will not give up. Pluto energy can also be called upon to ferret out any problems and to get to the bottom of things. Additionally, this energy is perfect for researching areas that are unclear, and for finding authoritative answers and solutions.

So now that we have looked at how cosmic energies work through the signs and planets, let's next analyze what we have learned from our experiment. Hopefully, you will agree that our basic premise of pursuing the goal instead of the money is feasible. Several important rules and suggestions surfaced and we will address them individually.

The first and most obvious rule is that if you want to successfully achieve your goal, you have to learn to take advantage of the available forces in your chart. If you haven't already done so, take a look at your chart and see what your strong points are. Identify which planets and signs are most powerfully located in your chart, and then figure out ways to use that strength to help you in pursuit of your goal. This is the simplest of the rules to grasp and the easiest to put into place.

Secondly, this experiment should have shown you that you don't have to start with a lot of resources to achieve your goal. You simply have to act on it. The act of acting produces its own results, and you will begin to see that something that initially began as only an act can eventually become a reality. The action must be physical and tangible. At first, you may only be able to do small things, but every step you take leads you to the next, larger step. As you begin doing things, others sympathetic to your goal will see your actions, and join in and contribute their specific energies and resources to the pursuit of the goal. As you goal begins to take on a life of its own, more and more resources will appear. The more energy and resources involved in the pursuit of the goal, the more likely the chances for success.

Additionally, the more resources you use, the more resources will be made available for you. If your resources are hoarded, then they will shrivel up and die. It is only by using them that you are able to make them multiply. If you have a large and lofty goal and are able to manifest the resources necessary to begin supporting that goal, and if you actually use those resources for the achievement of that goal, more resources will come to you to replenish the supply. It is a simple law of nature. Think about it. You know the old adage, "use it or lose it." If you stop pursuing your goal, if you lose direction or simply lose interest, then your resources to support the goal will dry up.

Finally, and this rule is not so obvious, your attitude about money, that is, the goal you select as representing money, can limit how much money or wealth you eventually create. How does your attitude limit your payoff? Your payoff will be commensurate with the size of the goal. If you have low goals, desires or aspirations, your payoff will be equally low. If all you aspire to is money for your basic needs, money for your personal security, money for your personal status or validation, then you are limiting yourself to that much money and no more. If, on the other hand, you want money and/or resources to do something a little larger than yourself, something with a more universal theme, or something for a lot of people instead of just one person, then it only stands to reason that the amount of money or other resources you would need would be larger. So if you are able to achieve a larger goal, then you are able to acquire larger resources in order to do it. What do I mean by a larger, loftier goal? Simply that you need to take a closer look at your present goal and see if it is the highest and most visionary that it could be.

In summary, then, we learned from our experiment that we could pursue our goal instead of pursuing the money through wise use of sign and planetary energies and through strategic action. We also learned that we could increase our resources by applying the resources we have towards the achievement of goal, not by hoarding them. And finally, we learned that the loftier the goal, the loftier the payoff. In order to have a larger and loftier goal, we must have a loftier vision. It is central to manifesting the large resources we have been discussing, and just as there are rules for pursuing your goal, there are specific rules and suggestions for raising the goal to a higher level, and this is the area that we will investigate in the next chapter.

CHAPTER 8

LEARNING TO VISUALIZE A HIGHER GOAL

Now that we are comfortable with the concept of pursuing the goal instead of the money, we are next going to look at how, by making a simple adjustment, we can increase the payoff, or the resources that we are able to attract. In other words, we will study strategies to increase the size of the wealth we produce by increasing or raising the caliber of the goal we are pursuing. The way to raise the goal is to make sure that it represents the highest and best version that it can be. The way to do that is to improve our powers of visualization, and in this chapter, we are going to learn how to do that.

Visualization is defined in the dictionary as the formation of mental, visual images, or the act or process of interpreting in visual terms or of putting into visible form. What does visualization have to do with uplifting our goal? The answer is that before you can raise it to its highest possible level, you have to be able to clearly see it. In order to manifest anything, you must first be able to visualize in your mind what it is that you want. The better you are at visualizing, the clearer your goal will be and therefore, the greater the chance that you will interpret it correctly and actually achieve it.

To be good in the art of visualization requires that you be able to paint a picture in your mind of the completed goal. This picture has to be correct down to the last detail. The more specific you can be, the better. For instance, if your goal is a new car, you need to be able to actually see yourself driving that new car. You should be able to describe the color, make and model, and the clothes that you are wearing as you are driving. If you goal is to eventually run your own business, you must be able to mentally see yourself running that business. Your business should have a name, and a location, and you should be able to see yourself sitting in your office at your desk, and if asked, should be able to describe the color of the walls and the location of the furniture. It is even helpful to be able to describe your feelings as you are sitting at your desk, running your company. Again, the more specific you can be, the better.

Some people are naturally better at visualizing than others, which of course, gives them a definite advantage when it comes to fulfilling their dreams. A lot has to do with the natal chart, and the placement of the visionary planets and the importance of the visionary signs. Later on in this chapter, we will analyze in detail the importance of the natal chart, planets and signs to the visualization process. However, right now, I want to continue to make some generalizations about the art of visualization and to show you that if you are not naturally good at visualizing, do not worry, for there are tricks you can learn to help you improve your skills.

One way to do this is through the wise use of the planetary energies you have at your disposal. This action alone can go a long way in helping you to better focus on your goal. Also, no matter how bad you think you are at visualizing, you can always improve the process through simple practice. Meditating on your goal every day with the intention of improving your visions can gradually make things become clearer. I know that some people do not have the kind of mind that normally sees things in pictures and colors; they may see things in geometric shapes or forms, or not see things at all. There are people for whom using the imagination is a struggle. But it can be done and all it takes is the intent to develop the skill and some effort on your part. And it is definitely worth the effort, because the importance of visualization cannot be overly stressed. As has been stated many times, once you are able to visualize what it is you want, you then have a much better chance of attracting it to yourself and there are many reasons for this. Let's take a look at a few.

First of all, if you have a clear idea of what it is you want, you will be better able to recognize opportunities. It only stands to reason that if you don't know what you want, or if you aren't quite sure because you haven't nailed down the details, then you may end up passing over what could have been a very lucrative or profitable situation. And, at the opposite end of the spectrum, you may waste your time and energy with people or in situations that are totally inappropriate to the furthering of your goal. But if you know what you want, you can pass over everything that is unsuitable, thus saving time and energy, and you will be able to quickly recognize those people and those situations that are supportive of and consistent with the achievement of your goal.

Secondly, if you are able to clearly picture your goal in your mind, then you are in a better position to present it to others who may be able to help you achieve it. Resources abound in the universe; the help that you need is out there, but in order to attract it, you must first be able to clearly identify what it is that you need. In order to do that, you must have a clearly defined goal in mind, a goal that you can easily articulate to others.

Third, once you can see your goal, you can then evaluate it based on whether or not it is in line with your life's purpose, and can make adjustments. You can't do that if you are just cruising along in life, taking things as they come. You need to know what you want, and then you can test it. If it doesn't work, you can make adjustments before putting your whole heart and soul into it. Remember, your goal has to be appropriate for you or it will not work. You may not even know what your life's purpose is right now, but by identifying goals and testing them, you will be going through the process of figuring out who you really are, for what we dream and envision says much about who we are. Astrologically speaking, your Ascendant will tell you a lot about your life's purpose, so your goal should be in line with the traits or qualities of your Ascendant.

This brings us to the next piece of our visualization equation. Our discussion so far has addressed the first half of the equation, namely, increasing our visualization skills. However, there is another part, and that is to ensure that our goal is the highest that it can possibly be. To do that, you must adopt a mindset that is as high as it can be. Then, the goals you visualize and the dreams you dream will also be at that high level. If you believe the axiom that says that you are what you think, it only follows that our dreams will reflect, both positively and negatively, our thoughts. The only way to adopt a high or lofty mindset is through practice. When you find yourself thinking negative, pessimistic, cruel or mean-spirited thoughts, remind yourself that you are trying to maintain a higher level and a broader perspective. This is, of course, not an easy thing to do, and you will find that you will fail quite often at first. But make the attempt. By making the attempt, you set yourself up subconsciously to try, and it is through the act of trying that we eventually achieve.

Before you begin thinking about your goal, make sure that you are mentally positioned in that high level mindset. It is futile to try to lift your goal to the highest level possible if you are not viewing the world and your place in it from a lofty perspective. If you have had a bad day, calm yourself for a while by meditating or thinking good thoughts before you begin contemplating your goal. You want to make sure that your mental attitude is receptive to higher rather than lower level energies.

Also, after you have formulated your goal, don't act on it immediately. Wait a few days and revisit it when you are again in a very calm and level frame of mind, just to be sure that you still see things in the same way. If your goal is the right one, nothing will be hurt by waiting a few days, or weeks, or even months to be sure that you are seeing and interpreting it correctly. If you revisit your goal a few weeks later and realize that it is not quite right, then you can try the visualization process again. Take your time. It is better to go slowly and get it right, rather than rushing into something only to realize after you have worked on it for a while that it is not what you really wanted.

Between your initial visualization process and the revisit, write goal-related thoughts down as they come to you during the day. Sometimes we receive profound insights and ideas when we least expect them. Also, pay particular attention to your dreams during this period. Our subconscious sometimes works things out and clears up questions through the dream process, so if you have an especially interesting or colorful dream, try to figure out if it has a meaning that might relate to your goal.

Once you feel certain that your goal is correct, and that it is the highest and best version, then you can proceed with the next step which is to embrace you goal with all of your being. You need to imbue your goal with all of the love and support that you can muster. If needs to become a part of you, and you need to dedicate yourself to its fulfillment. If you only half-heartedly embrace your goal, then most likely what you will achieve will be a half-hearted version. But if you adopt the attitude that you are going to succeed, that failure is not an option, then your goal will become a part of your every day life, and you will make decisions and take actions always with the goal in the back of your mind. You will start to "live" your goal, and each day you will make steady progress towards its fruition.

A word needs to be said about universal timing. Once you have completed the visualization process and are certain that your goal is correct and the highest and loftiest it can be, you will probably be in a hurry to get started. But bear in mind that the universe has its own time schedule for everything, and so sometimes even though you have the best of intentions, you may be required to just sit tight and wait. But if this happens to you, during the waiting period you can still be doing things that will help the goal along. Usually there is something that can be done related to the planning stages, and the more planning you do, the better. Astrologically speaking, the twelfth house is where we do the behind the scenes things, so check to see if you have transits involving that house which would give you help with doing background work. You can also use this time to devise contingency plans in case of emergencies or setbacks, or to network with others who you may need to call upon later when things really start rolling along. You can also use this time to revisit and redefine your goal. Sometimes the universe delays us from acting on our dreams or goals because our plans need to be tweaked, or perhaps something else needs to happen first before we can act. Whatever the reason for the delay, accept that it is necessary and appropriate, and use the time constructively.

This is where astrology can again play a key role. If you are forced to delay your plans, take a look at the transits and progressions in your chart, especially squares and oppositions, and see if you can ascertain the reason for the delay. Remember that squares will require that you overcome an obstacle of some sort, and oppositions usually require compromise or a meeting in the middle. Also, if any planet is retrograding, this may be another reason why your progress is stalled. Retrograde periods allow us to rethink decisions and plans and to make adjustments. Take a look at the area of your life being affected by the retrograding planet and see how that relates to your goal. For instance, Saturn is the planet of concretion, so if it is retrograding, then any project that we try to get off the ground will probably be stalled until it goes direct. While Saturn is retrograding, you can still be doing constructive things by looking over your plans and making any necessary changes.

This chapter is entitled "Learning to Visualize a Higher Goal" and hopefully you are starting to understand how everything we have discussed has been preliminary to attracting resources, for without proper visualization techniques, you cannot envision a lofty goal. Without a lofty goal, you have nothing to infuse with your heart and soul and then release into the world. Without a soul-infused goal to release to the world, you have nothing to attract the resources of others. That is the importance of visualization.

So now, let's take a look at our familiar representations of money, only this time, I want to look at each of them from the perspective of raising that particular representation or goal to a higher level.

MONEY AS POWER

Personal power or control over others, while very satisfying to our personal egos, is usually not very satisfying to the person or persons under our control. But power and control can be transformed into truly beautiful and beneficial objectives if the power is used in a positive and humane way. For instance, if it is used to help the weak defeat an evil or overbearing enemy, or if it is used to uplift and inspire others, or in some way to benefit a large group, then your goal of power can result in some very lofty achievements. I believe it was King Arthur who is attributed with the phrase, Might for Right," and if power is used to right wrongs, it is a legitimate, high-minded use of this energy.

There are many everyday examples of how power can be used to benefit others. You could decide to run for political office enabling you to use your political power to help reform Medicare or to make health insurance more accessible to all. On a smaller scale, you could use this goal to empower your school's PTA, or the local YMCA so that they can better serve the community. You could use your power as a tool to help others fight legal injustice, or you could lead a charge to oust a dishonest politician. You could use your power to start an organization that benefits others in some way, and run it with a fair and yet firm hand. Power used for the benefit of all is a truly noble goal.

MONEY AS SECURITY

Normally, this category sees money as representing personal security, and so the goal would be to acquire all of the safeguards that we traditionally think of as providing security, such as a home, a cupboard filled with food, a savings account, investments, etc. Lifting this goal to a higher level would require that we not think just in terms of our own personal security, or even the security of our immediate family. The idea of security must take on a larger significance. Neighborhoods, communities, cities, states, countries and finally the world all have to be included in this quest for security. Rather than concerning yourself with securing enough food just for your family, you might consider feeding all the children at the daycare center in a low-income neighborhood, or possibly becoming involved with feeding children on an even larger scale either through your own efforts or through contributions to organizations whose goal it is to feed hungry children. Instead of being satisfied with supplying a home just for yourself, you might think about how you can provide homes for many deserving families.

Whatever security represents to you should be shifted up a level so that it can represent security to a larger group. Ask yourself what you can do to make others feel secure in the same way that you feel secure and then try to formulate a plan to make that happen. This involves understanding that we as human beings, no matter what our status, country, religion, or nationality, all have the same basic needs and wants, and that security for one is security for all.

MONEY AS LOVE

Love is the quality that underlies everything in our universe, so having love as a goal is very beautiful aspiration. The way to raise this goal to a higher level is to make it more inclusive. Who and what you love has to shift from the personal to the universal. The emotional element has to be removed, for universal love does not discriminate; it loves all equally and impersonally.

To love in a bigger and more inclusive way, and thus raise your goal to a higher level, you might consider adoption or taking in foster children, thus allowing you to share your love with more people. Or, you may have an even bigger project in mind, such as opening an orphanage so that you would have many candidates to shower with your love. Or maybe you want to show love to the world by giving them your thoughts through writing and teaching, thus spreading the seeds of love in an intellectual way. Perhaps you would like to bake all the goodies that you love to eat and share them with the residents of a nursing home, and maybe eventually turning this into a large-scale project. If you like shopping for yourself, the next time you see something you really like, buy two and give one to your neighbor or a less fortunate friend. Make this a regular habit and you have turned it into shopping for love. There are many, many ways to raise the goal of love to a higher level, and they all start with the idea of inclusiveness, and that we are all one humanity, and that loving one is loving all.

MONEY AS SOCIAL STATUS

The goal of social status is a little trickier to shift to a higher level, for first we have to see how social status can benefit a larger population than just ourselves, and then find appropriate activities that will uplift and enlarge the goal. The trick is to stop looking for personal status and look for universal status. By that I mean, change the way you look at what gives status. Instead of looking at status as something given to you because of the things you own, or the people you socialize with, look at status as the things you can do that will benefit the world and humanity at large.

Status can be interpreted on many levels. Higher level status, the kind that will lift our goal to its highest possible level, has to be status that can't be bought with money. For instance, status could be gained through being the person who sells the most raffle tickets to a benefit for finding a cure for cancer, or being the person who actually organizes the benefit. Status could come from being included in the "in crowd" of the best teachers in your school because you give more to your students than is required. You status could come from being the person who gives the most time and energy to taking care of sick friends, relatives and neighbors. Set you sights on a status symbol of a high enough magnitude that it will benefit all of mankind, and the status you gain will be commensurate with the achievement.

MONEY AS VALIDATION

With this as your goal, personal recognition for one's value or contribution on the job, at home, etc., is extremely important. It should be very easy, then, to enlarge the goal by making one's value or contribution embrace a larger area. If you can contribute value in your personal life, you can contribute value in the world at large. Rather than working diligently for a single employer expecting a large salary or bonus, why not work diligently for a social issue or political cause. If you gained validation and personal recognition for being a good athlete, why not use your reputation to do something that will help others, and at the same time, increase your already good reputation. As your reputation becomes larger, the good you are able to do with it becomes larger, for your sphere of influence expands in direct proportion to your acts. Do something to promote peace in the world and, although you may not win a Nobel Peace Prize (which is a great example of personal validation raised to a high level), you will be recognized by those who benefit from your efforts. And who's to say that you won't someday win a Nobel Prize.

MONEY AS FREEDOM

Personal freedom is a beautiful concept. To be able to come and go as you please or to be free to choose the kind of work you do or don't do, are all very desirable and rewarding goals. If you start thinking about how to raise this goal to its highest level, it is obvious that you have to look at freedom from a broader perspective, one that includes bigger ideas and concepts, and one that would include a larger population than yourself. Pursuing the goal of freedom from a higher perspective could mean using your time and resources to aid the spread of human rights around the world. Perhaps you could become involved with the work of the United Nations, or maybe form an organization on your own which promotes freedom and human rights. Maybe your goal could be to show others how to develop personal freedom, through teaching them how to manage their time, or how to set goals and achieve them. The concept of freedom is vast and can be applied to every area of life, so it is simply a matter of finding the particular area you are interested in and developing it into a goal that will enable you to present your vision of freedom to a larger audience.

MONEY FOR MONEY'S SAKE: THE HOARDER

If this is your goal, you have a lot of work to do. By pursuing the goal of hoarding, you have created a virtual prison for yourself, because the quest for money, wealth and resources is a tiring and never-ending process. Before you can even think about raising your goal to a higher level, you must first re-define your original goal.

However, another option is available to you, an option that will save a lot of time. It is to simply adopt the opposite position from hoarding, that of money representing a tool of goodwill. This is the other monetary extreme, and since it is your exact opposite, in some instances, it may be easier to adopt it than to go back to one of the other previously discussed goals.

MONEY AS A TOOL OF GOODWILL

If you are starting from this point, then you are already well versed in the process of lifting goals to their highest level, for there is no higher goal than this. Visualizing money as a tool of goodwill and adopting that as your goal is the mark of a spiritually enlightened person, one who truly understands that all of us are connected and that it is our privilege and duty to help one another.

As the opposite position of the hoarder, this is a position of freedom. The person with goodwill as his goal will find each action rewarding. As resources are used to complete one goodwill project, a new one comes along to take its place, and a new set of resources appears.

Now that you understand the importance of being able to visualize, let's take a look at the signs that are best able to do this. For the signs that have more difficulty in visualizing, suggestions are offered for improving this ability. A particular sign is strong in your chart if it is your Sun or rising sign, or if you have a stellium of planets, i.e., three or more, located there.

ARIES

In most cases, this should be a good position for visualization, although some people with a lot of Aries energy in their charts may have difficulties in seeing anything past their own self-interests. If you are the latter type, allow yourself to imagine a goal that can be larger than yourself, one that you play a small role in accomplishing. Moving yourself and your personal desires out of the way will allow visualizing on the mental level to become a much easier process, and the goals should become clearer. Strong Aries types, so long as you make sure you are looking for the higher vision, should be able to see it in your mind and respond to it intuitively. Also, with your natural initiative and courageous response to new situations, it will be quite easy for you to take the next step, which is doing something to make the goal a reality. You are not afraid to act upon your instincts, so it is important that you have the proper mindset to allow your instincts to send you the best and loftiest message possible.

TAURUS

This is another very good placement for the art of visualization. It is quite easy for this sign to formulate and envision desires and goals for this is the energy that fosters strong desires. So if you are strong in Taurus energies and/or qualities, seeing your higher level goal is simply a matter of stepping up the nature of your desires. After all, a goal is merely a high level desire. Taurus, being an earth sign, is normally used to envisioning goals that are more earthy or materialistic in nature, but this tendency can be overcome if the intent to raise the goal is there. Those with Taurus prominent in their charts are also able to give their visions more life because they are able to infuse them with a large amount of emotional support, and emotional support is necessary to manifest any important goal. If you are not emotionally invested in your project, you will have a much harder time achieving it and gaining the support of others whose help you need along the way.

GEMINI

As a Gemini, you would most likely approach this idea of

visualization from a mental perspective, which actually works to your benefit. After all, the goal is to see the vision in your mind, and since you have a mental slant, that portion of the visualization process is quite easy for you. The Gemini mental aspect has to do with the lower or rational mind, so the actual visualizing takes place in higher, less concrete realms. But this Gemini energy is very important to the process because it allows for the translation of the goal or vision from abstract into more concrete language. Without this energy, you would have a hard time understanding your own vision, let alone explaining it to someone else. Gemini energy can also be very useful once the vision is grasped and understood and framed in words that can make the goal understandable. Gemini brings a light and airy feel to the operation, so instead of being tedious or boring, the process will be more lighthearted and fun than that experienced by others with heavier energies dominating their charts.

CANCER

This is actually a very good sign when it comes to visualization skills. The sensitivity of the Moon, which is closely related to Cancer, brings a strong intuition, so Cancer individuals can, if they choose, quite easily tap into their higher consciousness and envision a very high goal indeed. The problem that can arise sometimes with Cancer individuals is that they may find it difficult to separate themselves from mass thought so that they can have a hard time seeing their personal vision or goal. Because of the extreme sensitivity of Cancer individuals, it is very easy to lose yourself in the group mentality. And while compassion and sensitivity to others are admirable traits, the goal that you envision must be your own. Although it should have a higher, altruistic meaning, it must be personal and unique to you and your experiences, and come from your higher levels. If you are able to effectively separate your thoughts from the group mind, you have a very good chance of envisioning a very personal and yet very lofty goal that you can then put into practice for the benefit of many.

LEO

If you have a lot of Leo energy, your skills are naturally those of leadership, delegation and administration, more useful and therefore more active in the stages that follow the initial visualizing of the goal. You work best when someone else has seen the goal, and then gives it to you to bring to fruition. But our goal here is to help you learn how to develop visualization skills, and the best suggestion would be for you to look to your polar opposite, Aquarius, and bring their humanitarian outlook to life into the visualization process, which would enable you to see a goal where your personal wishes were not at the center. Then combine that with your legendary huge leonine heart, and you should be able to visualize a goal larger than yourself.

VIRGO

Visualization is always more difficult for those of you with strong earth signs in your chart, simply because you tend to live more in the concrete world, and visualization takes place in the higher mental realms. Virgo does give you the ability to clearly discriminate between the choices offered, and you are thus able to find the most appropriate goal. If, as you are doing this discriminating, you remember to make the most important factor the loftiness or height of the goal, then you should do well. The problem for you will be to lift your idea of what is important out of the material realm, and this may take some effort. Tempering your Virgo traits with other energies that are not so materially focused is probably the best way to go. Virgoan discrimination can be a great tool when it comes to visualizing the higher goal, but only if the focus of that discrimination remains at a high level.

LIBRA

Libra is one of the mental signs, so anyone with a lot of this energy would approach the whole visualization process from a totally mental perspective. The idea of weighing all of the facts so that an appropriate choice could be made would most likely be the method used to identify the goal. While not as visionary as some of the other signs, this energy can be used to make sure that the goal is in line with the law, that is, universal law as well as the moral law of the individual creating the vision. Libran energy is not really related to envisioning goals; it is in charge of the later process that ensures that we have made the correct decision. Librans gather all information pertinent to the goal, look at all sides of the issue and after much deliberation, make a decision. These are all steps necessary to the visualization process, but at the end, not at the beginning, therefore other energies will have to be called upon to formulate the original goal.

SCORPIO

Socrpionic energy is not usually helpful in the visionary process. This is because the sign itself is related to the idea of darkness due to its relation to Pluto and the underworld. This darkness is connected to the idea of going deep down into the psyche and identifying those negative traits that need to be brought into the light of day. This idea of bringing things out of the darkness into the light can be useful in examining our motivations once we have identified our goals, and thus can assist in eliminating weaknesses, faults, and incorrect assumptions. This energy can also be useful in helping us overcome negative emotions which hold us back, or undermine our intentions, but again, this is only useful after we have identified the goal. To be successful in the art of visualization, other energies will need to be used. Although Scorpios will not bring a lot of light to the process, they will bring a large supply of steadfastness and intensity that will aid the process of focusing the attention upon identifying the goal.

SAGITTARIUS

The optimist of the zodiac, this sign has no problem visualizing lofty goals. Sagittarian types are usually people with high moral or philosophical standards, and so their visions and goals would naturally include these higher principles. Sagittarians are normally very intuitive; they are well connected to the higher mind and can clearly see the direction in which they are to go. One thing that Sagittarians need to be careful of is the tendency to become so set in their views that they refuse to make any adjustments. Even the most lofty and beautiful visions can be improved upon, so ideas and suggestions from others, especially others that you know are also visionary in nature, should at least be considered before being dismissed.

CAPRICORN

Capricorn types are usually not known for great visionary skills, but generally have very broad perspective. This is a result of their natural inclination to climb to the top of their career or profession, giving them access to information that others on lower levels would not have. They can see the whole picture from where they stand, rather than just unrelated bits and pieces. Perspective is not the same as vision, but it aids in the visionary process. Perspective allows you to take into account all of the alternatives, and to see the results of choosing each one. The problem is that if you are using your gift of perspective to look at things from a totally materialistic viewpoint, it will be impossible to raise your goal to a loftier level. If you have a lot of Capricorn energy, you are well acquainted with the methods of achieving success; you just need to work on using those same methods to envision and achieve a higher goal.

AQUARIUS

This is the sign of the natural humanitarian, and thus one of the two signs most likely to visualize a strictly humanitarian goal, the other sign being Pisces. The last of the mental or air signs, at its best, this sign uses its mental energy to serve humanity. Remember that the symbol for Aquarius is the water bearer. According to Greek mythology, he served water to the gods on Mount Olympus. Visualizing something related to serving others, then, should be quite natural and appropriate for this sign. Aquarius is an intuitive sign, and it is also a humanitarian sign, but it is intuition and humanitarianism based upon logic and intellect. An Aquarian's goal will be crystal clear, broad in scope and vision, and tinged with a large dose of impersonal and yet universal genius.

PISCES

Being the last sign of the zodiac, those who are strong in Piscean energy have incorporated a little bit of each of the preceding eleven signs in their make-up. It is the reason Pisceans are so easily able to empathize with others. This can be both a blessing and a detriment.

On the negative side, it can keep you from being able to isolate your feelings from those of others. On the positive side, at least related to visualization, it allows one to truly dream and see all of the possibilities. If you can choose from all the possibilities the one dream that is truly yours, then you are on your way to realizing the dream. Also, being the most altruistic of all the signs along with Aquarius, the Pisces person is more likely to choose a goal that is on the higher turn of the spiral, one that will benefits others in some way.

Finally, we will take a look at the planets to analyze their strengths and weaknesses in the visualization process, and also how the energies of planets that are strong in your chart can be harnessed to help you arrive at your highest and loftiest goal. Remember that a planet is strong in your chart if it is angular, or aspects the Sun or the angles, especially the Ascendant.

SUN

The Sun, while extremely bright and powerful, is of more assistancc after you have discovered your goal than during the process of trying to define it. The Sun's energies will focus your attention and the attention of others on your vision, but it is not the planet that first sees the vision. The Sun functions more in the role of promoter; it can showcase the goal and allow you to present it in the best light. It can publicize what it is you are doing in a very beneficial way. The original goal, though, must be envisioned with the aid of other planetary energies.

MOON

The Moon can be quite visionary in nature, depending upon how you use its energies. If the Moon is powerful in your chart, you may have a tendency to dwell on the past, and to relate to every experience on an emotional level, including the experience of visualization. If you can step away from this tendency to go backwards, and instead use the Moon as a tool allowing you to see into the depths of your subconscious in a progressive way, you will be able to tap into the realm of idealism, rather than emotionalism, and it is here that you will find your true visions, dreams and goals, and be able to lift them to their highest and best state.

MERCURY

Mercury is very important in the mental portion of the visionary process. Mercury doesn't do the actual visualizing per se, but it is very much involved in the translating of the vision or goal from higher level, ethereal language to down-to-earth, rational language. Mercury interprets and sheds light on your goal, but you must have already seen it at higher levels, using energy of other, more visionary planets. If Mercury is strong in your chart, you can mentally describe something that you have seen in the intuitional realms. Without Mercury, your higher level goal or vision could be stalled in the upper realms, with no way to reach your rational mind.

VENUS

Venus will provide you with a lot of help in the visionary process, for you will be able to view your vision in the most beautiful and harmonious circumstances possible. Venus, known as the planet of love, will automatically give your visions a softer, kinder feel, which will make it easy to tap into the highest version of your vision. Venus, with its magnetic quality, will allow you to attract your ideal goal, and will enable you to recognize it because of its beautiful form and because, with a strong Venus, you can see beauty as well as exemplify it. Therefore, not only will you be able to see the highest form of your goal, but you will also be able to attract help and resources from others.

MARS

While this energy is not especially visionary, nor is it good in the art of visualization, a strong Mars can give you the energy and vitality to want to figure out how to do it. You will have to look to other energies in your chart to give you more assistance in the actual visualization process, but a little Mars enthusiasm can carry you a long way. Mars is known for its aggressive tendencies, so you can use this energy to aggressively pursue your goal once you have formulated it. Remember that this energy must be tempered by more visionary energies, otherwise you will find yourself aggressively pursuing all kinds of ideas and activities, none of which will amount to anything.

JUPITER

If you are blessed with a lot of Jupiterian energy in your chart, you are very fortunate as far as your ability to visualize is concerned. You will instinctively be able to see the highest and best in everything, and so you can carry this skill over into other activities including visualization. You will take a very spiritual approach to the art of visualization and as a result, your visions will necessarily be of a high, altruistic nature, full of love and hope. Jupiter is strongly related to your true spiritual path, so your dreams, goals and visions will all tend to lead in the direction in which your soul wants you to travel.

SATURN

Saturn, because of its tendency to want things fixed and concrete, is more likely to be a hindrance rather than an aid in the visionary process. Saturn will try to keep you firmly planted on the ground, making it difficult to pull visions out of the clouds. You probably have a hard time imagining anything because your thought process is so strongly based in reality. Strong Saturn types will need a lot of help from other energies, especially those transmitted by Uranus, Neptune or Mercury.

URANUS

This energy is excellent for aiding and supporting the visualization process. Although more intuitive than visionary in nature, intuition is closely tied to vision, as both relate to bringing ideas and impressions from the higher mind into the lower, rational mind. Uranus, though, will give the impressions a fresher, more revolutionary appearance. Visions with a Uranian flavor will be ahead of their time, and may take some initial effort for you to understand them even though they are your own ideas. Whatever your basic vision, Uranus will spice it up, and will assist you in your quest to raise your goal or vision to its highest level.

NEPTUNE

Of all the planets, this is the best one for visualization, so if Neptune is strong in your chart, you are probably very good at formulating pictures and concepts in your head. As a matter of fact, if you have a lot of Neptunian energy, you may find that you spend too much time in your head, living in imaginary situations, rather than living in the real world. The trick with Neptune is to learn to use the energy from the highest level possible, and then anchor it on the ground by attaching the idea to something concrete in your life. It helps if you have a strong Saturn in your chart, or a lot of planets in earth signs. If not, you must work at finding a place in your life where you can apply your Neptunian visions in a positive, tangible way.

PLUTO

Pluto is, as you know, famous for being able to bring hidden issues to the surface, and if you apply this trait to the visualization process, this energy could be used for unmasking hidden desires, dreams and goals that have been lurking in our subconscious. Pluto can also help eliminate those goals that are either no longer appropriate because they have fulfilled their purpose, or that are holding you back and keeping you from seeing your true direction. Also, once you have discovered your true path or passion, this energy is excellent for instilling the willpower and total commitment necessary to carry the dream to fulfillment.

CHAPTER 9

THE MIDAS TOUCH & OTHER MONETARY LESSONS

The concept of money has weighed heavily on the minds of men over the ages. It has been the subject of any number of books, movies, and popular songs. Themes regarding money and its pursuit can be found in many historical, biblical and mythological stories. While they are only "stories," there is much truth to be found in them. Here are a few stories, parables, or myths that I think are worth considering in our study of money.

THE MIDAS TOUCH

This is probably the most famous of all the mythological legends about money. When we say that someone has the Midas touch, we mean that they are able to turn anything they are involved in into a profitable situation. However, if we dig a little deeper, we will see that there is a much more basic meaning to the story. Turning everything into gold may not be the smartest idea, for there are certain things that just shouldn't be gold plated. The story goes as follows.

Dionysus, the god of wine, had a tutor and favorite companion named Silenus. Silenus was a satyr, half man and half goat. One day, a very intoxicated Silenus lost his way and stumbled upon the palace of King Midas. The king treated Silenus with graciousness and hospitality. When Dionysus found out about the king's kindness to his friend, he offered to grant King Midas one wish as a reward. Despite being advised against it by Dionysus, King Midas wished that everything he touched would be turned into gold, believing that being the richest man in the world would bring him happiness.

Initially, the king was quite happy as he went around turning everything in his palace into gold, but the foolishness of his wish quickly became apparent. Everything, including the food he tried to eat, was transformed into gold. He even turned his young daughter into gold when he tried to hug her. Finally, starving and in total despair, King Midas begged Dionysus to relieve him from his unwise wish. Dionysus obliged, and told the king to wash himself in the river Pactolus, thus ending the curse. The king also washed his daughter in the river, thereby returning her to life.

So what is the moral of this story? The obvious one is the foolishness of equating money with happiness. A deeper moral might relate to the idea of taking the easy way out, of getting something for nothing, and the importance of earning your riches, that is, having done something to merit them, or having them represent something such as your life's goal or quest. If money represents the goal or vision, to wish for money for its own sake is therefore doomed to failure. To King Midas, money represented happiness, but he didn't pursue that goal; instead he pursued the outer trappings, and found, after looking a little closer, that the underlying meaning was not the same. And just in case you missed the message that King Midas showed very poor judgment, there is another story about him related to a mistake in judgment resulting in his ears being changed into ass's ears. King Midas was not a very wise man, so let's not follow his example.

JOB: BIBLICAL MONEY LESSONS

I'm sure you are at least vaguely familiar with the story of Job in the Bible, but I will give you a refresher course, just in case you have forgotten how it goes.

Job was a good man, a family man, and a financially wealthy man. He and his wife had ten children. Job was going along thinking everything was fine. Then one day, God and the devil had a conversation. The devil told God that the only reason Job loved him was because God had blessed him with material wealth. So God told the devil to take everything away from Job and see what happened.

Initially, Job did not complain after losing all his children and his money, although he was in great pain. So God allowed the devil to heap even more disasters upon him, plaguing him with boils and other physical ills. After all he had endured, Job began to wish that he had never been born, threw a few temper tantrums, and did a little cursing, all understandable, given his situation.

Job commiserated with his friends, who believed that he had lost everything because he had done something to lose favor with God. His friends counseled him to curse God. Finally, though, a young man named Elihu came to Job and told him that he was being tested by God, that he had not done anything wrong, and that he should stop the tantrums and just be patient. Elihu, it turned out, was correct. Job calmed down, and made amends. Eventually he was given back everything that had been taken away from him and more.

It is never stated exactly why all of Job's wealth was taken away from him, other than that it was a test of some sort, so what is the lesson that we learn from Job's trials? Perhaps it is that his wealth was not related to his moral character. He was a good man and yet his wealth was taken from him. Money is not related to goodness. It is related to other things, and the following story may shed some light on what those other things may be.

MATTHEW CHAPTER 25: THE PARABLE OF THE TALENTS

Here is another Biblical story full of imagery and symbolism. The basic story is as follows.

A man, just before departing on a trip, called in his three servants and doled out his property to them. To the first servant, he gave five talents, to the second, two talents, and to the last servant, one talent. The servant given the five talents went out into the world and used his talents and doubled them, so that he now had ten talents. The servant with the two talents also went out into the world and used his talents, so that he ended up doubling his talents as well. But the servant who was given only one talent decided to bury his talent in the ground and not use it.

When the man returned from his journey, he asked for an accounting from each of his servants as to how they had used their talents. The two servants who had used and doubled their talents were praised, and were given more talents as a reward. The servant who had buried his talent, though, was rebuffed, and his one talent was taken away from him and he was cast out into the darkness.

The symbolism here is obvious. During the time of Jesus, a talent was a valuable sum of money. The current meaning of talents, though, that of gifts and opportunities bestowed upon us by the universe, is appropriate as well in understanding the story. Equating money with talents or gifts is a perfect graduation in meaning. Our talents and abilities are where our energies should be focused, so that we can perfect them and use them in a way that benefits others. By so doing, we increase or multiply our talents, and in the old sense and the new sense, we gain both in talents and in wealth.

JACK AND THE BEANSTALK

This is a very well known children's tale, but in case you have forgotten the details, here is a recapitulation.

Jack and his mother were very poor. They lived in a little cottage and were nearly starving. So Jack's mother decided that the only way they could make it through the winter was to sell their only cow. Jack was entrusted with the task, and so set off to market to sell the cow. On the way, he ran into a butcher who talked Jack into trading the cow for some magic beans.

When Jack returned home and showed his mother the magic beans, she was so angry, she threw the beans out the window. The following morning, the beans had sprouted into a vine that reached all the way into the clouds. Jack decided to climb the beanstalk to see where it would take him.

When Jack reached the top of the beanstalk, he saw that he was in a very different land. There was a large castle in front of him, but before he had a chance to investigate it, a fairy accosted him and told him that the castle once belonged to his father. His father, she explained, had been a very kind knight, but had been killed by a very mean giant who now occupied the castle, and the giant now claimed all of Jack's father's belongings.

Jack ventured inside the castle and met the mean giant's wife, who hid him because otherwise, as she explained, her husband would eat him. From his vantage point, Jack could see the giant and some of his possessions: the goose that laid the golden eggs, the talking harp, and the bag full of gold pieces. On separate nights, Jack stole the possessions from the giant while he was sleeping, first the goose, then the gold pieces, and finally the harp. As he was grabbing the harp, due to its gift of gab, the harp alerted the giant to what was going on. The angry giant chased Jack down the beanstalk. However, Jack reached the bottom first, cut the stalk, and the giant crashed to the ground and was killed by the fall. Due to Jack's exploits, he and his mother now had plenty of money and would never have to starve again.

This folktale is believed to be several hundred years old, with many versions, although the basic story remains the same. The theme of ascending to the heavens or clouds has been around for ages. In this story, though, the central message is that one should seize the opportunities presented to him, that is, to climb the beanstalk. When our hero, Jack, does climb the beanstalk, his fortunes change. Had he been afraid to climb it, or had he simply been uninterested, his life would have remained the same. In fact, in the version of the story presented by Andrew Lang in *The Red Fairy Book*, the fairy actually tells him as much:

"You showed an inquiring mind and great courage and enterprise, therefore you deserve to rise; and when you mounted the Beanstalk you climbed the Ladder of Fortune."

The other lesson that Jack teaches us is that if you pursue opportunities as they arise, you just may discover your talents, or what is rightly yours. Jack had no idea of his background until he ventured out into the world, climbed the ladder of fortune, and met the fairy who told him he was the son of a knight and that the treasures which the giant had were rightly his. We cheered for Jack because he was able to defeat the mean giant, but more importantly, he rose to the challenge of life and won.

JUNO (JUPITER'S WIFE) AND MONEY

This isn't so much a lesson about money as it is a mythological connection to money. The word "money" comes from the French word "moneie" which comes from the Latin word "moneta." The derivation of this word comes from the goddess Juno. As you may or may not be aware, Juno, in Roman mythology (Hera in Greek mythology) was the wife of Jupiter (Zeus). Juno was the most powerful of the goddesses. She had many duties, each with an associated title. She was known as Juno Regina, which related to her role as protector of the Roman people. She was also called Juno Lucina, relating to her role as goddess of women and children. Another of her names was Juno Moneta, referring to her role as the advisor of the Roman people, especially in advising those about to marry. In ancient Rome and even earlier in Greece, the word "moneta" meant an advisor, or one who warns or one who makes people remember. It is in this role as advisor that the myth of Juno Moneta developed relating her to money.

Legend has it that one day, a flock of sacred geese in a sanctuary of Juno's on the Capitoline Hill squawked the alarm that saved Rome from an invasion of the Gauls in 390 B.C. A temple was built in honor of Juno Moneta on the hill in gratitude for having been warned of the attack. About one hundred years later, the first Roman mint was built adjacent to Juno's temple, and the coins were initially struck with the head of Juno Moneta on the face. They were called "moneta," hence the connection to the word money. The word "mint" also comes from the Latin word "moneta" due to this story, as the word "mint" means a place where coins are made.

What can be extracted from this story regarding the meaning of money? Perhaps the meaning is as simple as the origination of the word. But perhaps there is a deeper meaning. In astrology, the asteroid Juno deals with committed relationships, due to the fact that she is the goddess of marriage. Another possible interpretation, then, of her relationship to money would be a physical sign of a commitment to a partnership, or a symbol of the strength of the commitment to a joint cause, purpose or mission.

So what can we glean from all of these stories about money and our relationship to it? First of all, we learned how not to behave if we want to be wealthy. King Midas taught us that money does not buy happiness, and that if money is the goal in itself, that is, if it is not the representation of some goal or of some talent we possess, then it will bring only bad fortune.

Second, we learned from Job that we don't have money simply because we are living a good and righteous life, for his wealth was taken away from him, even though he was good and righteous. Being good and living a righteous life are wonderful things, but wealth is related to other factors.

Third, we learned from the parable of the talents that if we use our god-given talents to aid others, they will increase, and so will our wealth. How do we learn what we are to do with our talents from astrology, so that we can increase them and thus increase our wealth? We look at the sign on our Midheaven. The Midheaven represents our calling in the world, or our work for the universe, so to speak. If you are confused about what you are to do with your life, meditate on the meaning of your Midheaven and you should receive insights about where you should be showcasing your talents in the world. Also, look at the sign and house that hold the ruler of your Midheaven for additional clues. Make sure that you study the placement of your North and South Nodes as well, for they are related to your calling because they give you an idea of the direction in which your life should be heading. The South Node, remember, relates to areas that you have already mastered, and the North Node shows you the areas you need to begin developing.

Next, from Jack we learned that even if we don't know right now what our talents are, or what is rightly ours, we must pay attention to the opportunities that are presented to us, for the universe has a way of letting us know who we really are, and we need to have the courage to seize our futures. Astrologically, how do we learn what our talents are? By looking at the trines in our natal chart, because these represent energies that flow easily in our lives and, as such, are areas where we can excel. We can look at the house and sign position of our Part of Fortune as well. The Part of Fortune represents that area of our life that brings us the most joy and fulfillment, because usually this is the area where we are the most talented.

And finally, from the story about Juno Moneta, we not only learned the origin of the word "money," but we also learned about how money is related to the idea of commitment to a joint cause or purpose. One person committed to and pursuing a noble cause is great, but two is even better. If you are in pursuit of a noble goal and you have combined your energies with a partner or partners also committed to the goal, your chances of success increase. The amount of good you are able to do multiplies as the number of people involved in the goal multiplies. The wealth gained is in proportion to the size of the effort, which gains in might and strength as the number of people involved grows. A mighty effort reaps mighty rewards!

CHAPTER 10

RE-CALCULATING YOUR WEALTH QUOTIENT

We have come a long way in our pursuit of wealth. Now, in this final chapter, we are ready to take another look at our Wealth Quotient, only this time, we are going to look at it from the perspective of the concepts we have learned in the second half of this book. That means that we are going to create a new Wealth Quotient that takes into account the premise that money equals what it represents to us. We will be measuring our ability to visualize and achieve our goal, or the representation of wealth. After computing your new Wealth Quotient, you can compare your score with some individuals who I believe have very high Wealth Quotients from this new perspective.

Our new Wealth Quotient takes into account the following factors:

A. How good are we at visualizing goals, and are they as lofty as they should be?
B. Can we bring our goals out of the clouds and verbalize them so that others can see the vision also?
C. Do we have enough pioneering spirit and desire to energize the goal?
D. How good are we at actually manifesting a dream or idea or goal? Can we make it a reality?

As you can see, we are valuing slightly different traits than we did with our first Wealth Quotient test back in Chapter 3. Attraction qualities are not as important as is the ability to visualize a lofty goal and then pursue it. This new Wealth Quotient measurement implies that if the goal is lofty enough and if enough energy is applied to make it manifest, then the wealth and/or resources will naturally follow.

The planets that are included in the new Wealth Quotient calculation are the ones that are the most important in visualizing, energizing and then materializing the goal. They are Neptune, Uranus, Mercury, Mars, Jupiter and Saturn. I will not go into a long discussion about them because we have already covered their roles in visualizing, energizing and materializing goals in Chapter 8. Neptune allows you to see clearly the highest and most ideal vision, Uranus "electrifies" the vision and changes it from ordinary to revolutionary, and Mercury allows you to interpret the vision, so that you can communicate it to others. Mars energizes the vision, Jupiter holds it to the ideal, and Saturn allows you to give it form.

The signs that are most important in the new Wealth Quotient are all related to the planets listed above, and so their contributions are similar, and we have already discussed them at length as well in previous chapters. The signs are Pisces, Aquarius, Gemini, Aries, Sagittarius and Capricorn. Pisces and Aquarius are selected because they are the most altruistic of the twelve signs, and would therefore be the signs most likely to choose a goal that was humanitarian and compassionate in nature. Gemini is the sign of communication, aiding in the interpretation and communication of the vision to others, Aries provides the initiative to get a project off the ground, Sagittarius gives the one-pointedness to stay focused on the goal, and Capricorn gives the perspective, steadfastness and discipline to see the project through to completion.

The houses that are the most important in the new Wealth Quotient are again related to the planets and signs outlined above. I will, however, give a little discussion of why each of the houses was chosen. The houses are the eleventh, twelfth, third, first, ninth and tenth.

ELEVENTH HOUSE

This is the house of hopes and wishes, also of friends and group activities. For the longest time, I could not see the connection between hopes and wishes, and friends and groups. It finally dawned on me that perhaps the connection had to do with the fact that our most elevated hopes and wishes involve others, not just ourselves. Any goals or visions perceived here would therefore stand the greatest chance of being created in an altruistic and universal light.

TWELFTH HOUSE

This is the house where we are most closely tied to our subconscious mind, and to our highest ideals and visions. Related to the sign Pisces and the planet Neptune, the twelfth house allows the visions and ideas generated by Neptune and in the sign Pisces to find a place of expression in your life. A strong twelfth house will "house" the vision safely until it is ready to be taken to its new location.

THIRD HOUSE

The third house is the house of communication, so planets and aspects related to verbalizing and interpreting the goal would blossom here. This is the house where you can receive and decipher all kinds of spiritual messages. Without this place from which to interpret, communicate and disseminate the things learned from Neptune and Uranus, lofty ideas would be stuck forever in an ethereal mist or fog.

FIRST HOUSE

Related to the sign Aries, this is the seat of your individuality, your spark of life and your vitality. Planets placed in the first house are vitalized by your inner spirit, and therefore have a much greater chance for positive expression. Everything is energized in the first house, so naturally a goal or vision directed from this house would be full of life and able to hold its own as it was transformed from merely a vision into a final realized project.

NINTH HOUSE

This is the house ruled by Jupiter, thus related to Sagittarius. It is the house that holds our highest spiritual values, our highest ideals, and our quest. This is where we get on the visionary path and do not deviate from our goal. Having a strong ninth house, then, will put us in the right place to insure that we stay headed in the right direction in pursuit of our new, loftier goal.

TENTH HOUSE

If we want our goal or vision to manifest in the world, then this is the house it should be in, for the tenth house is the most elevated house in our chart and relates to what we put out into the world. Our vision should be strong and powerful and placed high for all to see. This house is where we would look to find our worldly success, so placing our goals in this house will give them an excellent chance to succeed.

Now we're ready to take the new Wealth Quotient test. You will note that in this test, I have divided the five categories into sections so that you can score each section separately if you wish. All of the categories are important in order to successfully bring your goal to fruition, so this will allow you to identify in which categories you are strongest and weakest.

Rules:

The rules are the same as in the first Wealth Quotient test, but I will repeat them here.

1. You are allowed a maximum orb of ten degrees for conjunctions, seven degrees for trines, sextiles, squares and oppositions, and three degrees for semi-sextiles and inconjuncts.

2. If more than one planet placement or aspect is true for any one item, you may allot the points for each. For instance, if having Neptune or Uranus in the 10th house is worth 20 points and you have both Neptune and Uranus in the 10th house, then award yourself 40 points.

The New Wealth Quotient Test

Section I: Ability to Envision a High Level Goal

1.Neptune and Uranus are in aspect	25 pts
2.Neptune or Uranus in Aquarius or Pisces	20 pts
3.Neptune or Uranus in the 11th or 12th house	20 pts
4.Neptune or Uranus rules the 11th or 12th house	20 pts
5.Ruler of 11th or 12th house in 11th or 12th house	20 pts
6.Ruler of 11th or 12th house in Pisces or Aquarius	20 pts
7.Ruler of the 11th or 12th house in aspect to Neptune or Uranus	20 pts
8.Any planet other than Neptune or Uranus in the 11th or 12th house	5 pts
9.Any planet other than Neptune or Uranus in Aquarius or Pisces	5 pts

Section II: Ability to Interpret the Vision or Goal

1.Mercury in aspect to Neptune or Uranus	25 pts
2.Mercury in the 3rd house	20 pts
3.Mercury in Gemini	20 pts
4.Mercury rules the 3rd, 11th, or 12th house	20 pts
5.Ruler of 3rd, 11th or 12th house in aspect to Mercury	20 pts
6.Ruler of 3rd house in 3rd house	20 pts
7.Ruler of 3rd house in Gemini	20 pts
8.Neptune or Uranus rules the 3rd house	10 pts
9.Ruler of 3rd house aspects Neptune or Uranus	10 pts
10.Neptune or Uranus in 3rd house	10 pts
11.Neptune or Uranus in Gemini	10 pts
12.Ruler of 3rd house in 11th or 12th house	10 pts
13.Ruler of 3rd house in Pisces or Aquarius	10 pts
14.Any planet other than Mercury, Neptune or Uranus in the 3rd house	5 pts
15.Any planet other than Mercury, Neptune or Uranus in Gemini	5 pts

Section III: Ability to Energize the Vision or Goal

1.Mars in aspect to Mercury, Neptune or Uranus	25 pts
2.Mars in the 1st house	20 pts
3.Mars in Aries	20 pts
4.Mars rules the 1st, 3rd, 11th or 12th house	20 pts
5.Ruler of 1st, 3rd, 11th or 12th house in aspect to Mars	20 pts
6.Ruler of 1st house in 1st house	20 pts
7.Ruler of 1st house in Aries	20 pts
8.Mercury, Neptune or Uranus in the 1st house	10 pts
9.Mercury, Neptune or Uranus rules the 1st house	10 pts
10.Mercury, Neptune or Uranus in Aries	10 pts
11.Ruler of 1st house in 3rd, 11th or 12th house	10 pts
12.Ruler of 1st house in Gemini, Pisces or Aquarius	10 pts
13.Ruler of 1st house aspects Mercury, Neptune or Uranus	10 pts
14.Any planet other than Mars, Mercury, Neptune or Uranus in the 1st house	5 pts
15.Any planet other than Mars, Mercury, Neptune or Uranus in Aries	5 pts

SECTION IV: Ability to Stay Focused on the Vision or Goal

1.Jupiter in aspect to Mercury, Uranus or Neptune	20 pts
2.Jupiter in the 9th house	20 pts
3.Jupiter in Sagittarius	20 pts
4.Jupiter rules the 1st, 3rd, 9th, 11th, or 12th houses	20 pts
5.Ruler of 1st, 3rd, 9th, 11th or 12th house in aspect to Jupiter	20 pts
6.Ruler of 9th house in 9th house	20 pts
7.Ruler of 9th house in Sagittarius	20 pts
8.Mercury, Neptune or Uranus in 9th house	10 pts
9.Mercury, Neptune or Uranus rules 9th house	10 pts
10.Mercury, Neptune or Uranus in Sagittarius	10 pts
11.Ruler of 9th house in 1st, 3rd, 11th or 12th house	10 pts
12.Ruler of 9th house in Aries, Gemini, Pisces or Aquarius	10 pts
13.Ruler of 9th aspects Jupiter, Mercury, Neptune or Uranus	10 pts
14.Any planet other than Jupiter, Mars, Mercury, Neptune or Uranus in the 9th house	5 pts

15.Any planet other than Jupiter, Mars, Mercury, Neptune or Uranus in Sagittarius — 5 pts

SECTION V: Ability to Manifest the Vision or Goal

1.Saturn conjuncts the Midheaven	25 pts
2.Saturn in the 10th house	25 pts
3.Saturn in Capricorn	20 pts
4.Saturn in aspect to Uranus, Neptune, Mercury, Mars or Jupiter	20 pts
5.Saturn rules the 10th house	20 pts
6.Ruler of the 10th house aspects Saturn	20 pts
7.Ruler of the 10th house in the 10th house	20 pts
8.Ruler of the 10th house in Capricorn	20 pts
9.Neptune, Uranus, Mercury, Mars or Jupiter conjunct the Midheaven	20 pts
10.Neptune, Uranus, Mercury, Mars or Jupiter in 10th house	20 pts
11.Neptune, Uranus, Mercury, Mars or Jupiter in Capricorn	20 pts
12.Ruler of 10th house aspects Neptune, Uranus, Mercury, Mars or Jupiter	10 pts
13.Ruler of 10th house in 1st, 3rd, 9th, 11th or 12th house	10 pts
14.Ruler of 10th house in Aries, Gemini, Aquarius, Pisces, or Sagittarius	10 pts
15.Any planet other than Neptune, Uranus, Mercury, Mars or Jupiter in the 10th house	5 pts
16.Any planet other than Neptune, Uranus, Mercury, Mars, Jupiter or Saturn conjunct Midheaven	5 pts
17.Any planet other than Neptune, Uranus, Mercury, Mars, Jupiter or Saturn in Capricorn	5 pts

Now that you have taken the test, here are some astrological charts of individuals who have been successful in achieving high and lofty goals. Their scores on the new Wealth Quotient test are given, so you can compare your score with theirs. If your score is high and you feel that you haven't really accomplished anything yet in your life, go back and re-read Chapter 4 in which we discuss how timing is an important factor in realizing goals. If your score is lower than you think it should be, then re-read Chapter 5, where we give suggestions on how to improve your score. Also, note whether there is one area that you excel in but others areas in which you are weak. If that is the case, you may not have been able to accomplish anything because, as pointed out earlier, skills in all five of the categories are necessary to bring a goal to fruition. If you scored particularly low in one category, you might want to consider looking for someone to work with who is strong in the categories in which you are weakest.

Finally, realize that taking the first step towards your goal is the most important thing you can do to assure future success. You can think about your goal all you want, but until you actually do something to make it real, it is only a dream. The first step can be as simple as sharing your vision with your spouse, or as elaborate as visiting your local bank to discuss financing. It can be signing a lease on a building, or simply giving your project a name. A name, after all, goes a long way towards making something real. If you know what to call it, it is no longer just a dream. Many actions will qualify as a first step; you just need to pick one and do it.

Gandhi had a vision of freeing India from British rule through the concept of non-violent resistance. He has Uranus conjunct the Midheaven and sextile Jupiter, square Neptune and semi-sextile the Moon, ruler of the 10th house. The 10th house ruler is in the 10th house. The Sun, ruler of the 11th house, is in the 12th house. Mars squares the Moon, trines Uranus, and opposes Neptune. (Oct. 2, 1869 NS, Porbandar, India, 7:11:48 am LMT)

New Wealth Quotient: 480

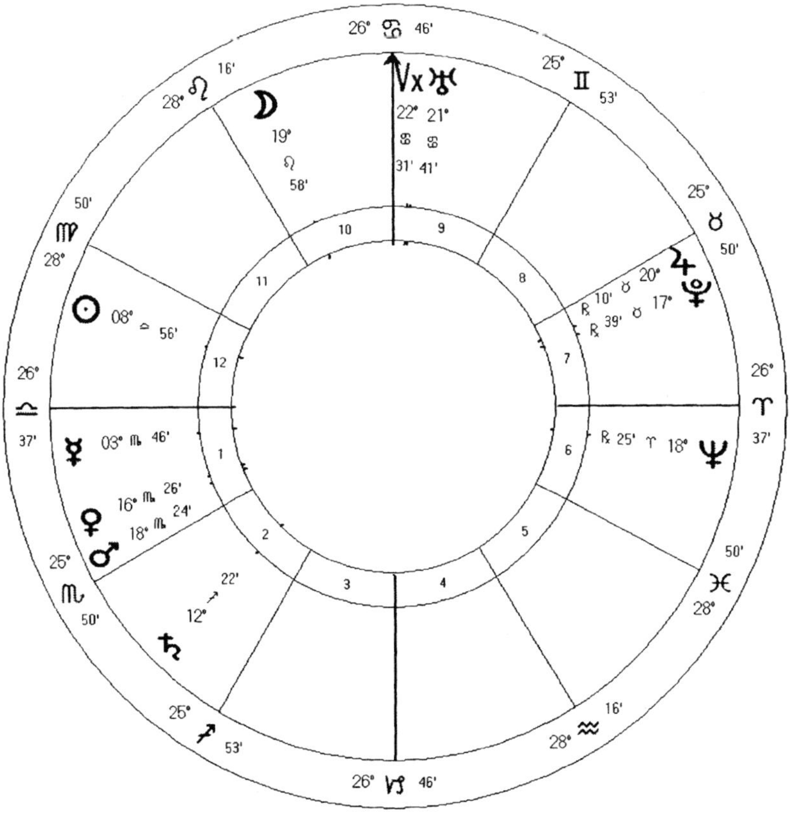

Eleanor Roosevelt had a vision of making basic human rights universal. She has Uranus, Mercury and the Midheaven conjunct and Mercury semi-sextile Venus, ruler of the 10th house. Mars is inconjunct Saturn and opposite Neptune. Pluto, ruler of the 11th and 12th houses, trines the Midheaven, Uranus and Mercury and squares the conjunction of Venus and Jupiter. The Sun is in the 10th house. Saturn squares Uranus. (Oct. 11, 1884 NS, New York, NY, 11:00 am EST)

New Wealth Quotient: 490

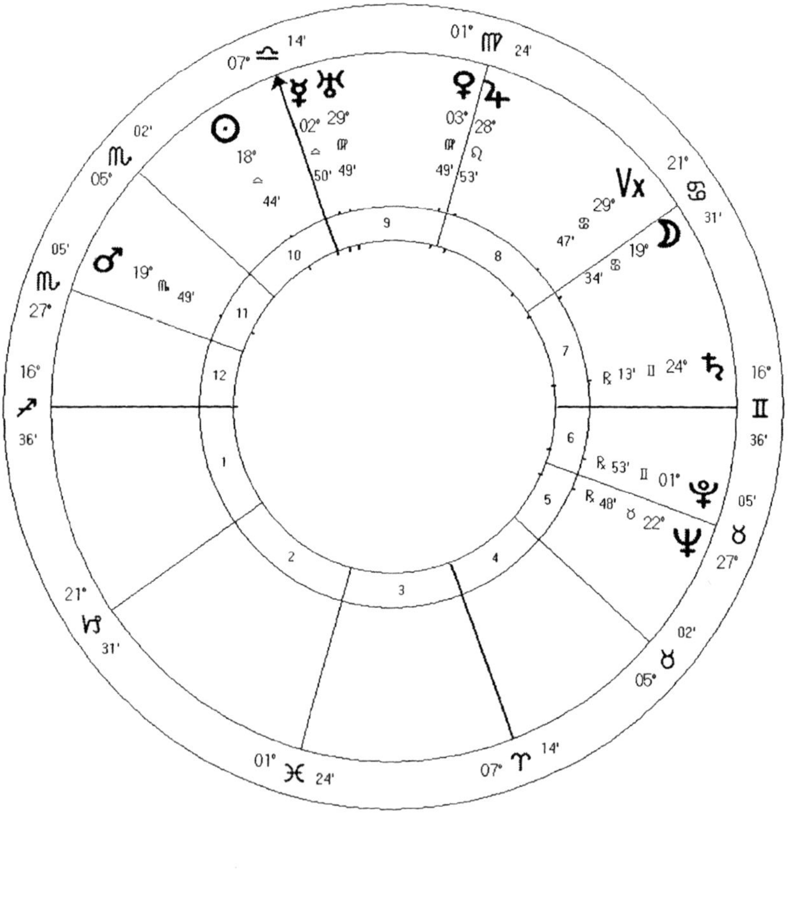

Martin Luther King, Jr. had a vision of fighting for equality for African-Americans through non-violent protests. His Sun conjuncts the Midheaven and Uranus sextiles it. Mercury is in the 10th house. Saturn semi-sextiles the Sun and Midheaven. Neptune trines Saturn. Uranus, the 11th house ruler, is in the 12th house. Jupiter squares the Midheaven and semi-sextiles Uranus. (Jan. 15, 1929, Atlanta, GA, 12:00 pm CST)

New Wealth Quotient: 490

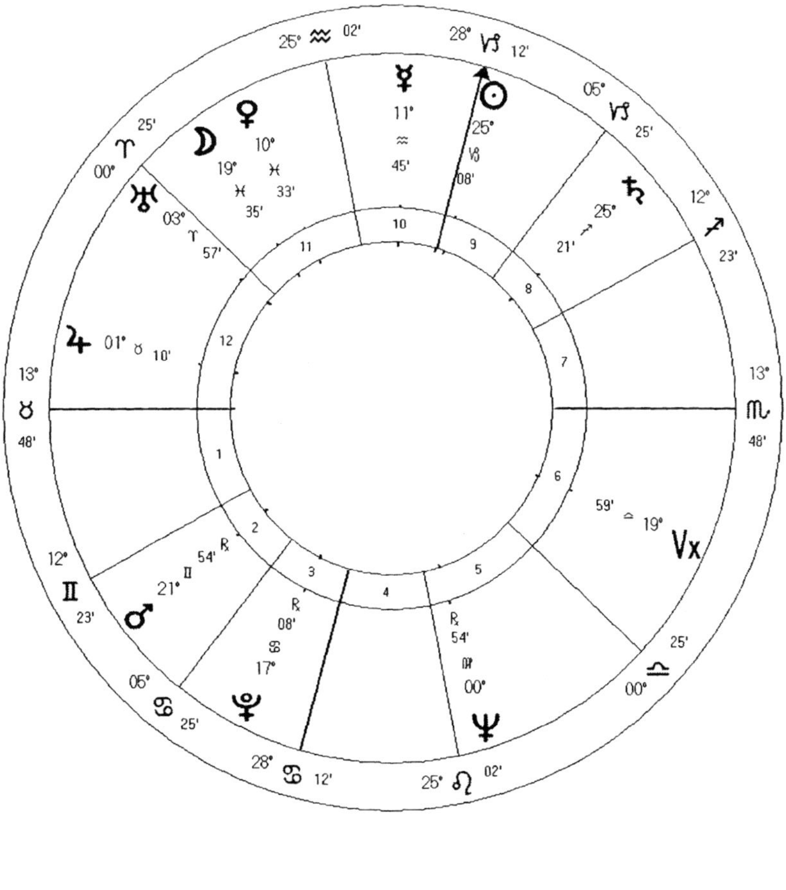

Mother Teresa had a vision of feeding and caring for the needy in India. Jupiter, the 12th & 1st house ruler, conjuncts her Midheaven. Uranus opposes Neptune, and both square her Midheaven and Jupiter. Mars semi-sextiles Jupiter. (Aug. 27, 1910, Skopje, Yugoslavia, 2:25 pm MET)

New Wealth Quotient: 480

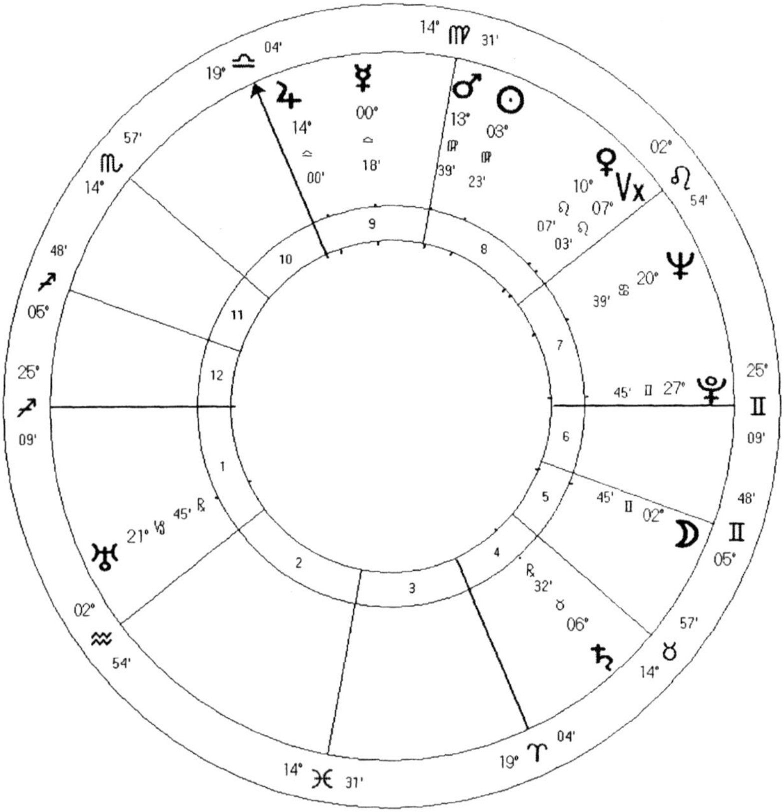

Abraham Lincoln had a vision of abolishing slavery while preserving the Union. Neptune and Saturn, the 12th house ruler, conjunct his Midheaven, and Uranus semi-sextiles Neptune. Mercury squares the Midheaven, Neptune, and Saturn, and trines Uranus. Jupiter, the 10th and 11th house ruler, inconjuncts Mars. (Feb. 12, 1809 NS, Hodgenville, KY, 6:54 am LMT)

New Wealth Quotient: 535

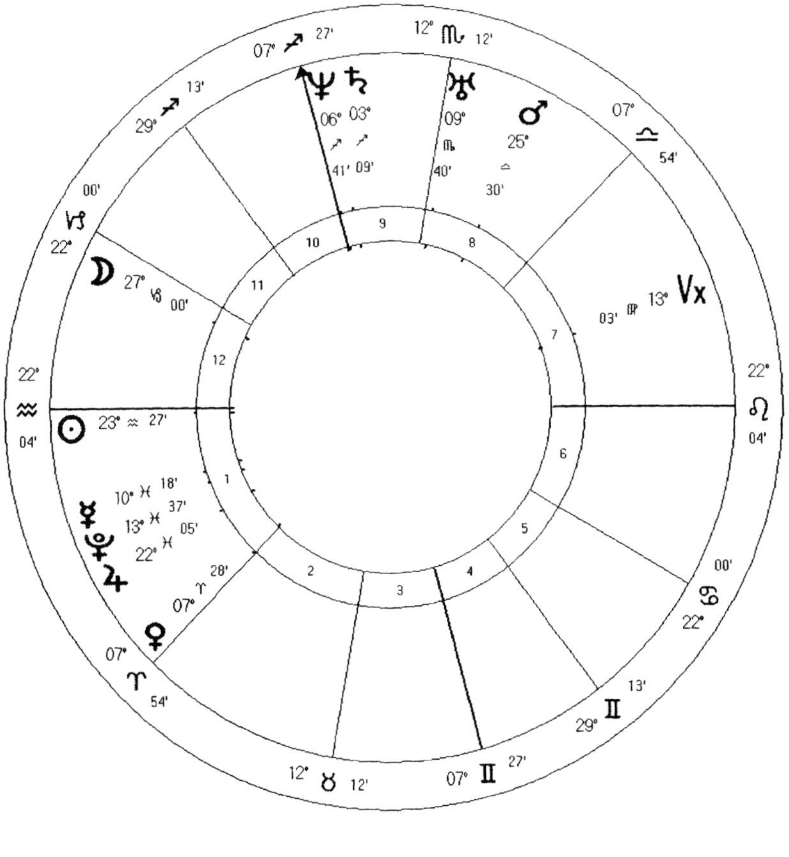

SOURCES

Braha, James, *How to Be a Great Astrologer*, Hermetician Press, Longboat Key, FL, 1992.

Columbia Encyclopedia, "*Money*," 6th Edition, 2001.

Doty, R.G., and Stanley Fischer, "Money," *World Book Online Reference Center*, World Book, Inc., 2004.

Hickey, Isabel, *Astrology: A Cosmic Science*, CRCS Publishing, Sebastopol, CA 1992.

Lofthus, Myrna, *A Spiritual Approach to Astrology*, CRCS Publishing, Sebastopol, CA 1935.

Perowne, Stewart, *Roman Mythology*, Peter Bedrick Books, New York, 1969.

Sakoian, Frances and Acker, Louis, *The Astrologer's Handbook*, Harper & Row Publishers, Inc., New York, 1973.

ASTROLOGY & MONEY: ***What's Your Wealth Quotient?***

Order Form

Please Print:

Name____

Address____

City__________________________**State**_______________

Zip__________________

Phone (   )____________________

_______**copies of book @ $12.95 each $**__________

Postage and handling @ $1.50 per book $__________

Total amount enclosed $__________

Make checks payable to TLH PUBLISHING COMPANY

Send to:
TLH PUBLISHING COMPANY
1845 Cambria Avenue
Landers, CA 92285